Acting Honestly

Acting Honestly:

A Handbook and Reference Guide for Actors

Tesia Nicoli

United States MMXII

All rights reserved. No part of this book may be reproduced or transmitted in any form without the explicit permission in writing from the author. Photocopies may be made for the actor to use in practice. Monologues, scenes, and one act plays may only be performed in classroom settings or for auditions. None of the material contained in this book can be produced or performed for a paying audience without explicit permission from the author. Brief passage quotes from this book are permissible when used in the context of reviews or articles.

Manufactured in the United States of America.
Published in Allentown, Pennsylvania

Copyright © 2012 by Tesia Nicoli

ISBN-13: 978-1479381753
ISBN-10: 1479381756

Designed by Tesia Nicoli

Printed in the United States of America.

To my Jared, Jada, and Alexander for constant patience, love, and understanding. For believing and encouraging...

And...

To all the souls who inspired this book ~ your ambitions, passions, and love of the art feed mine.

CONTENTS

SECTION I: Acting Principles................................7
   1. Introduction..9
   2. Conquering Stage Fright...........................12
   3. Paths to Relaxation and Relieving Tension...........20
   4. The Art of Communication in Acting....................25
   5. A Little History: Teachers and Methods..................34

SECTION II: Getting Started................................39
   6. Refining Monologues and Scenes Through Exercises..41
   7. Memorization......................................47
   8. General Notes for Auditions............................50
   9. Performance Evaluations.................................71

SECTION III: Elements of Acting............................79
   10. Warm Ups & Games......................................81
   11. Emotions and Conflict..................................95
   12. Character Development................................111
   13. Get in Touch with You..................................125
   14. Listening...128
   15. Free Your Imagination and Creativity..................131
   16. Improvisation..137
   17. Use Space..145
   18. Concentration...148
   19. Additional Thoughts, Advice, and Quotes.............151

SECTION IV: Monologues, Scenes, and One Act Plays 155
   20. Monologues..157
   21. Female..157
      Jess from *Tomorrow*
      Lainie from *Modern Romance*
      Kathy from *Promise Me*
      Greta from *Smashing the Pumpkins*
      Emilianna from *Everywhere and Nowhere*
      Stella from *Smashing the Pumpkins*
      Gramma J from *Get Gone*
      Greta from *Smashing the Pumpkins*
      Ally from *Get Gone*
      Kate from *Smashing the Pumpkins*

22. Male..175
    Peter from *Smashing the Pumpkins*
    Gary from *Circumlocution*
    Ben from *Smashing the Pumpkins*
    Ron from *Burning Money*
    Vince from *Get Gone*
    Roger from *Roger's Big Bad Day*
    Alan from *Smashing the Pumpkins*
    Jake from *Patience of Hate*
23. Scenes..187
    Everyday Dribble
    The Ladies Room at Comet Cave
    Everything Pink
    Abandon and Illness
    For a Good Cause
    Spats
    Am I Evil? Yes I Am
24. One Act Plays..211
    On Candleswick Avenue
    In the Swing Line

Glossary: General Acting Terms..............................221
Stage Directions..228
Recommended Reading List...................................229
Bibliography..230
Acknowledgements...232
About the Author...233

SECTION I: ACTING PRINCIPLES

INTRODUCTION

Acting can be fun. Don't let it get around.

— Sanford Meisner

    Chances are that you already know a thing or two about acting. If you haven't already been performing, you've certainly watched plenty of television, movies, and theatre. Observing the art of acting gives you personal insight into the world of acting. Whether you are a novice or an experienced actor, this information will be useful to you. The more experienced actor may find some of this book to be a refreshing review, but will also discover new techniques to take their current talent to a new level. If you are even remotely dazzled by the intriguing world of acting, then this book will serve as a handy resource.

    This book is divided into four sections: Acting Principles, Getting Started, Elements of Acting, and Monologues and Scenes. The first three sections offer inspiring quotes, advice, exercises, and materials to help you better understand the craft of acting. The last section offers material that you can practice with. What makes this book different from any other acting book is that it cuts to the core of what acting is and gives you a wealth of tools to enhance your skills.

    Acting is an art. Keep in mind that great actors are labeled "great" through opinion only. It is impossible to please all of the people all of the time. As much as it pains me to admit, there probably are some people out there who think Meryl Streep is a terrible actress. And, as much as I disagree with that, they may have their reasons to support that opinion. You will have people critique your talent as you travel down the road of the actor. When others tell you what they think of your performances, listen to what they say. Collect opinions from as many people as you can. Really take to heart what *most* of them seem to agree on. Take everything else with a grain of salt. If you believe you truly have what it takes to be an actor, then fight for your dream. Take classes, learn, observe, practice, prepare, immerse yourself in every way you can - and just keep going.

This book is a compilation of years of diverse training, valuable experiences, and thorough research. Relevant information from a wide array of classes, workshops, auditions, books, and experiences have been organized into this handbook. When I started acting, this was the book I was looking for, but it was nowhere to be found. When I started teaching acting classes in 2006, I started to organize all of my notes and memories. The result makes up the core of this book. I hope that you'll find this book to be easy to follow and valuable to you as you pursue acting in your life.

Is it possible that you'll have a thriving career as an actor? Sure. Is it probable? Well, most of us will never win an Oscar. Most of us will never star in a commercial film with a two hundred million dollar budget. But many of us have the acting bug. Many of us have the curiosity to know what it is like to lose yourself in a character. Many of us just want to learn how it all works or have a desire to come out of our shells. This book will give you the facts in simple terms.

Throughout this book the term "actor" will be used to identify both an actor and an actress. I also refer to the actor as a male. Examples will reference "he" and "his". I feel it makes reading easier and less distracting to not switch back and forth between genders.

After reading this book, you should be able to: find ways to relax your mind and body before a performance, have a variety of useful exercises to use to develop characters and enrich scenes, understand how to access your emotions on a believable level, know how to fully connect with your character, be prepared for auditions, and grasp refined acting skills for all facets of performance.

CONQUERING STAGE FRIGHT

I read a thing that actually says that speaking in front of a crowd is considered the number one fear of the average person. I found that amazing – number two was death! That means to the average person if you have to be at a funeral, you would rather be in the casket than doing the eulogy.

– Jerry Seinfeld

    The day I decided to pursue acting was the day when my desire to get on stage was greater than my fear of performing in front people. Fear kept me behind the curtain for a long time. That being said, it is logical to conclude that if your fear is too strong, you may never be able to shake it. Fear (at least in the context that we're going to discuss it) is a weakness in mental strength.
    I remember going to my first community theatre audition. It was for *A Christmas Carol*, as well as a new play by a local playwright. My nerves almost made me back out of auditioning, but luckily I brought two supportive friends along with me. I felt optimistic that

I'd land a role, since I was auditioning for two shows at one time. But I wasn't prepared for handling the intensity of my nervous energy while performing. Nor did I have a clear idea of how to express and project myself on stage. During the audition I knew things weren't going smoothly but felt helplessly stuck. The director gave me several opportunities to re-read the lines. Each time he'd say, "Okay, do it again, but this time really fill up the room!" I'm fairly certain I performed it the same inhibited way every single time. It was nothing short of a disaster. As a result, the entire experience practically gave me a heart attack. At the time I hadn't had any prior experience or training, but I desperately wanted to act in theatre (even after that less-than-average audition). It was extremely difficult getting through that first audition experience. However, that very experience gave me the drive to continue, and fueled me forward. I (obviously) didn't land a role from that first audition, but I immediately enrolled in a class. A few classes later, I went to my second audition and won my first role in community theatre.

Fear of speaking and acting in front of others is a natural reaction. Your apprehension may never completely disappear, but you can learn to control it. Those who dabble in theatre enjoy the exhilaration of performance. The "acting bug" as it is often called is contagious and fun. Once you're over your fear, you'll be thankful you took the plunge. With some understanding of stage fright, as well as some tips on curbing your fears, you will soon be able to control your anxieties.

Everyone including accomplished actors and professional speakers experience a degree of stage fright and they all use that energy differently. In a way, nervous energy is a gift. After all, it *is* energy. You just need to teach yourself how to funnel it into a productive energy that would benefit your character and not hinder you. The best way to harness that energy is to practice wielding it.

My first acting class helped me enormously with controlling and understanding my stage fright. I clearly remember my instructor's first words to the class, "Who has a monologue they want to perform?" I was completely unaware that we had to have a monologue for the class. But half of the class raised their hands. I was shocked. And they were volunteering! I had thoroughly read the class description, and it made no mention of needing a prepared monologue. Then I watched as my world went from black and white to every color of the rainbow. Student after student went up in front the class and transformed themselves into characters. They all appeared to shed their fear and put themselves out there. They were completely vulnerable. I finally understood that *that* was what this was all about. Taking a risk and leaving your inhibitions behind. Giving yourself permission to let go, get out of your own way, and get lost in someone else. I now had a full understanding of what the director from my first audition meant when he said, "Okay, do it again, but this time really fill up the room!" Seeing what all of these other actors were doing opened up my eyes. The instructor put each of them through extensive and specific exercises to get a desired result. And the results were breakthroughs! Those students had the same desire in their hearts as I did. I finally gave myself permission to let go. That class changed me and my entire approach to acting. That was the point in time when I realized that fear and stage fright were part of the process, and I had to find a way to control it and use it.

It's possible that stage fright stems from an ancestral beginning. Theories suggest that stage fright stems from not wanting to be singled out of a "pack."

Historically speaking, humans are social animals and live in groups like a families or clans. These groups take care of its members. If a member of the group behaved undesirably in the other's judgment, then that person could be banished. Abandonment would result and survival would be a lonely and difficult road. Was it the survival of the fittest, or survival of the ones who fit in? Certainly this "outcast" sensation makes one feel vulnerable.

Your first questions regarding stage fright might be: what is physiologically happening during a stage fright experience? Basically adrenaline is released – which has been typically related to the fight or flight reaction. Adrenaline can be useful, but when it's released in excessive amounts, trouble begins. The more you perform, the more you'll be able to control this release of adrenaline and use it more effectively. Lots of actors enjoy this "energetic" feeling since it sharpens their senses and makes them feel more alert and alive.

Here is How Your Body May React:

- Heart rate increases
- Blood vessels contract
- Pupils dilate
- Digestion and other processes can slow down or temporarily stop
- Rate of breathing increases
- Blood glucose rises
- Medullae is stimulated to produce epinephrine & norepinephrine

Common Symptoms of Stage Fright:

- Closed throat
- Dry mouth

- Sweating
- Shakiness
- Trembling jaw, lips, and/or mouth
- Nausea and upset stomach

Breathing eases stage fright. Slow, even breaths send a soothing message to your central nervous system, and in turn your adrenaline levels will decrease. If you can slow down your breathing, then your nerves will settle.

Keep positive messages in your head: "I can do this" or "I am talented." It may feel silly to say these things to yourself, but the payoff is worth it. Repeating positive messages will build your confidence.

Mistakes happen. Chaos will ensure. This happens in any and every aspect of life, not only in the theatre. It is expected. But always keep in mind – there are no mistakes if you choose not to show them. They can edit out the mistakes in film and television. During live theatre, you just have to ad-lib a little bit, get back on track, and then let it go. You'll be surprised at how capable you are at bouncing back.

It may be hard to believe, but your nervousness isn't written on your face. Actors don't appear nearly as nervous as they really feel. If you ever get the opportunity to record your acting on video, you'll probably be surprised by the result. In a public speaking class during college, I gave a speech on dreams. Despite being fully prepared to do my speech, all I heard my inner-voice telling me was how boring the speech was. I felt awful. When I watched the video later, I was shocked at my composure. I had great posture, I annunciated, and I made perfect sense. All of those negative thoughts in my head hadn't visibly surfaced.

Ever wonder why you can recite your monologue perfectly at home but, then when you get up to perform it for an audience, it comes out quite differently? Your nerves and your body are reacting to fear. An actor can learn to identify this change and fine-tune it to work to their advantage. As with anything else, you have to *practice* this skill before you will feel results.

When I was struggling with a very difficult and controversial monologue by Eve Ensler, the director gave me notes on how to improve. On the last rehearsal, he didn't say a word. Just before the show, I approached him and asked, "How was my monologue this last time?" He put his hand on my shoulder and said, "When you're out there, you'll feel the energy. You'll sense the audience and all of their energy, and you'll play off of that." He was right. At that point in my acting career, I never really thought about how much a live audience could intensify the energy level of a performance. My live performance of that monologue was better than of any of my rehearsed ones.

Here are some tips you can try to help you conquer stage fright. Not all may work for you, so try different methods to see what benefits you the most.

In Preparation for an Audition or Performance:

- Take a class or find a coach to guide you.
- Be well prepared.
- Dance with your eyes closed to a favorite song.
- Listen to inspiring music.
- Exercise or meditate – both can ultimately benefit mental well-being.
- Make sure you give yourself enough to time. Don't rush to your performance; but don't pace idly around. This allots you too much time to dwell on your nervousness.

- Steer clear of alcohol or caffeine before performing.
- Don't eat if you aren't hungry.
- Sing to relax before the event.

Just Before the Audition or Performance:

- Show up early.
- Pick up on any cues around you (scripts, cold-reading sides, sign up sheets, character synopsis, forms to fill out, etc.).
- Talk to others around you. Engaging in conversation will help distract you from your nerves.
- Look over any notes or lines you may have.
- Look at photos that make you happy.
- Breathe slowly, steadily, and deeply into your lower abdomen.
- Stretch your whole body; particularly your back, neck, shoulders, and jaw.
- Situate yourself into a different position if you start shaking.
- Take a quick, brisk walk to rejuvenate yourself.
- Sip lukewarm water.
- Yawn.
- Think about a moment when you feel at peace with yourself and feel your connection to the world.
- Shake hands and smile with others.
- Go somewhere private to relax and warm up.
- Go find a mirror and check to see how you look.

Strategies for When You're Up on Stage:

- Tell yourself, through affirmations, that you are good at acting.
- Imagine that you are just talking among friends.
- Picture the audience applauding, laughing, and listening intently.
- Project yourself and fill up the space around you with your voice and emotions.
- Don't hold any papers over your face.
- Feel free to briefly chat with the auditors (if the opportunity presents itself) or make a joke after your performance, to ease your heart.

Keep This in Mind:

- You're on stage to have fun – and, more than likely, so is everyone else.
- Once you're up there, your fear usually goes away.
- What's the worst that can happen?
- It's completely normal to feel nervous.
- Even if it isn't a great experience, you'll know you've tried.
- Take control of that nervous energy and use the adrenaline to your advantage.
- Focus on the task at hand and let everyone else fade into the background.
- No one expects perfection.
- No one ever died from stage fright.

PATHS TO RELAXATION AND RELIEVING TENSION

Acting is relaxation for me. I enjoy it more then directing or teaching because I don't have to argue with myself.

— Lee Strasberg

Nervousness means that we are concerned with ourselves rather than with the things we need to do.

— Lee Strasberg

    Tension is an actor's enemy. Once you truly know yourself and where you store your tension, you will be able to quickly rid yourself of it. Quick methods to release tension are: yawning, stretching, and "working out" areas where you store tension (i.e. doing head-rolls).
    After really exploring my body for tension, I found that my jaw was almost always a hot spot. Other areas that seemed to personally hold concentrated tension for me were in my shoulders and legs. I found that sitting very still in silence while slowly searching for tension (starting at the top of my head and ending with my toes) worked very well. If I found any tense

areas while searching, I would exercise that spot until the tension was loosened. Now that I am familiar with my problem areas, I can easily locate tension and will it away.

Tension can also manifest itself in speech. If you ever find yourself tongue-tied, or perhaps your mouth is running faster than your thoughts, you can try saying "Buh-Duh-Guh," over and over. This exercise will warm up the front, middle, and back of your mouth.

The key to being relaxed for any performance is to be as prepared as possible. If you're not prepared, you can't help but be nervous. Preparation provides you with the confidence you need to get through the audition or performance. As a result, you can purely focus on your performance.

Relaxation will help you to be more open with your character and fresher with your performance. Take, for example, a string instrument. If the strings are too tight, they won't have the true, free-flowing sound as if they were adjusted just right. Relieve the tension, but keep your performance alive and energetic with adrenaline.

The relaxation exercises listed below can be adapted until you come up with your own process. Don't feel constricted by these exercises. Be creative and use what best works for you. Remember - what works for one person isn't always what works for everyone.

EXERCISES:

Head-To-Toe Relaxation

First, sit in a chair and get as comfortable as you can. Close your eyes. Explore your body for tension, imagining the tension as a liquid. Imagine the tension slowly flowing out of your feet. Start by concentrating on the top of you head. Explore your scalp, your forehead, your eyes, your entire face, and then gradually go into your neck. Search for tension everywhere and let it flow down and away. Continue to gradually explore your whole body from the top down.

Take as long as you'd like for this exercise. Some people like to take thirty minutes or more to really relax. Other actors choose to take only five to ten minutes.

If you find an area that is especially full of tension, you can tense that area for a few seconds and then release it. Another great idea is to "breathe into" areas that hold a lot of tension.

In the last moments of this exercise you should search for any lingering tension. Check your problem areas. Then, tense your entire body and hold. Will away any remaining tension. Look for it, identify it, and will it to flow out of the bottom of your feet when you release. When you are done open your eyes, give a mighty yawn, and a good stretch. You should feel refreshed and comfortable!

Rag Doll Reach and Drop

Find an open space in the room where you are at arms length away from anything else. Reach up into the sky. Keep reaching and stretching…as if you are reaching for an imaginary rope just out of your grasp. Reach equally with each arm. Stretch and reach! After a minute, try for one last reach of that imaginary rope, and then drop forward from the waist. Arms should be hanging lifelessly in front of you. Very slowly move to a standing position by imagining that there is a string pulling you upright, one vertebra at a time. Take your time doing this. When you are completely upright, let your head rest on your chest. Slowly do head rolls to the left five times and then to the right five times. Alternate head rolls a few more times and then slowly raise your head. Finally, yawn and stretch.

Imagine On-Your-Own Relaxation

To start, find a comfortable position and close your eyes. Pick a scenario to relax yourself. Select any activity that relaxes you and makes you happy. Several scenarios are listed below. Try to let go of other thoughts. The goal is to really concentrate on your scenario. You may want to play relaxing music to accompany this exercise.

- Imagine that you are a hawk soaring through the sky. You can soar effortlessly. Feel free to land on top of a tree branch and take in the view of the rainforest, or soar in circles around a waterfall. Explore this gift and get lost in your surroundings.
- Imagine that you are in a paradise of your own choosing. No one is there to disturb you. This place is completely your own. Explore it, lie down, or take in the wonder through your own eyes. For example - you could be on a yacht at sea, exploring your old childhood bedroom, in the desert at sunset, up high on a mountaintop, walking through the forest, or on a deserted tropical island.
- Once again, imagine that you are alone. Picture yourself in a place where there is no gravity. How would it feel to move? How would you use your arms and legs to propel yourself?
- Imagine yourself as a creature of the deep ocean. Explore the other sea life and take in its wonder.

Be sure to focus on what it feels like to be submerged. Take into account the temperature, the pressure, and how you must move to get around.

Once you are completely relaxed and truly lose yourself in your scenario, slowly open your eyes. Be sure to give yourself a good yawn and stretch.

Quick Relaxation in Chairs: Feeling Physical Presence

Find a comfortable seated position. Close your eyes. Explore your body to find tension. Find at least three tense parts of your body. Tense up these individual areas and then release. Do this several times until the tension diminishes or disappears. Finally tense up your whole body and release three times. Each time, pushing the limits of how long you can hold the tension. Then explore how your body feels, sensing any external influences.

Notice the temperature of the room. Do you feel a slight breeze? How does the cloth from your clothing feel against your skin? The waistline of your pants? The collar around your neck? The watch on your wrist? The chain around your neck? Your shoes? Is anything overly constricting? Is anything too loose? Is anything too hot? Is the skin on your hands too dry? Are your lips chapped? Again tense and relax your whole body, one last time. Open your eyes, stretch, and yawn.

THE ART OF COMMUNICATION IN ACTION

The most important things are the hardest to say, because words diminish them.

— Stephen King

I don't think you're ever going to be much of an actor if you're not observant — studiously observant — particularly of people in life.

— Morgan Freeman

COMMUNICATION AND ACTING

  Studying human communication can help to get to the root of acting. There is not a person alive who couldn't benefit from improving their communication skills. Communication is quite often taken for granted. Clear communication can be more difficult to get across than you'd realized. Here are some interesting facts about communication:

- Most communication is not intentional.
- Ninety-three percent of communication is nonverbal.
- Your chances of an early death are two to three times higher if you lack in strong relationships.
- We define who we are by the way we interact with others. Our identity stems from our relations with others. If we didn't communicate with others, we would lose our sense of identity.
- The experiences we have as a child are the most significant and substantial identity shapers of our lives.
- Maslow's Hierarchy of Needs* puts communication third – only after safety needs and physical needs.

Those facts put so much weight into shaping any character you are portraying. You can begin to ask yourself certain questions about your character just based on these facts. Such as:

- How social is your character?
- What behaviors of your character are intentional? And which behaviors are not intentional?
- How much does your character communicate verbally and nonverbally? In what ways does your character communicate nonverbally?
- Does your character have any strong relationships? How many? With whom?

* Maslow's Hierarchy of Needs (1968): Psychologist Abraham Maslow placed human needs into five categories. *Physical* – air, water, nourishment, sleep, reproduction; *Safety* – protection from threats to our personal security; *Social* – communication and social needs; *Self-esteem* – the urge to feel like a valuable person; *Self-actualization* – to become our maximum potential or the best we can be.

- What type of people does your character choose to communicate with?
- What experiences did your character have in childhood?

With acting, you want your character to be consistent in personality and emotion, but remember that we all adjust our behavior around different people. The way you speak to your grandmother will be different than the way you speak to your friends. While your character may be consistently sarcastic to their spouse, would they behave that way to their employer? Real-life communication is the basis of all character performances.

Here are more criteria to consider when building your character:

- What behaviors he possesses.
- How he adapts his behavior when speaking to certain characters.
- The involvement he wants to have in a particular situation.
- The degree of empathy and understanding that he conveys to other people.
- The solutions, advice, support, etc. that is offered to the receiver(s).
- How his self-monitoring is shaping the situation at hand.

A high self-monitor possesses a good sense of what he's saying, how he's communicating, and how the receiver is reacting and feeling about the encounter. If your character has a low self-monitor, he will give much less attention to the reaction that his behavior creates. Low self-monitoring gives the feeling of "what you see is what you get".

Understand that who your character is and how he conceives his self-worth is through the perception and judgments of those around him, as well as the perception of himself in comparison to those around him. Without having others around him to define who he is, he'd have nothing to compare himself or standards to conform with.

Your character has both a "private" and "public" self. When he is "private," he is being the person he wholly and honestly is to only himself. When he is "public," he is being who he wants to appear to be to others. It is important to realize that your character has multiple identities as a parent, a teacher, a student, a co-worker, a neighbor, a customer, etc. An example of this is in the film, *My Week with Marilyn*. When we see Marilyn Monroe (played by Michelle Williams) interact with Colin Clark, she is free, open, playful, moody, and honest. But when we see her interact with her fans, she puts on a constant façade.

Remember that there is a core person within your character that carries values, morals, and beliefs in everything he does.

The playwright establishes some of your character's personality traits. You will get some information about the character through descriptions and dialogue. Some of the information about your character is inferred and, whenever there is an absence of information, you must use your imagination to fill in the blanks. We will explore character building more in the Character Development section of this book.

NONVERBAL COMMUNICATION

Nonverbal communication includes your tone of voice, body language, and the nonverbal sounds you make. The actor has the authority to determine his character's nonverbal behavior. Verbal communication is simply the very words you speak. The playwright has already supplied the direct verbal elements along with some basic direction. Vocal communication is the sound and tone that comes out of your mouth. Therefore, nonverbal communication can be vocal, just not verbal.

All behavior has a value with or without the use of words, but can be ambiguous due to its nonspecific nature. Nonverbal communications work better expressing feelings than showing a preference or an idea. For instance, it is much easier to show that you are upset by shedding tears or collapsing onto the sofa or stamping your boot down hard on the floor through nonverbal communication than it is to convey the brilliant ideas your character has for his new business.

Your character will strive to get others to see him the way he wants to be seen through the way he behaves, how he appears, and the things he surrounds himself with. As your character evaluates others, they are doing the same in return. In this type of exchange, it can be easy to misunderstand the nonverbal cues.

Most of the messages we send are not completely truthful. How often have you led someone on to believe that you liked something much more than you actually did? When you are portraying a character you must act honestly, yet mislead as your character would. It comes down to being honest with who your character is and how humans behave.

There are unlimited nonverbal choices you can make as an actor. Some things may be in the script and the director may dictate others, but the actor can decide many of them. Types of nonverbal communication include:

- **Facial expressions** - how much eye contact to give your partner, whether to wrinkle up your nose with disapproval
- **Physical movement** - how to move you body (fidgeting, slouching, tilting your head)
- **Touching** – a hug, a pat on the back, or a smack on the head
- **Vocal tone** – intonation, how loudly or how softly to deliver a line for punctuation, how much time to use to deliver a line
- **Proximity** - how close to get to your partner's face when you're feeling threatened or how closely to sit next to a distant relative to view old photos
- **Presentation** physical attractiveness, the things you surround yourself with, a mustache, wearing an expensive suit, or wearing bright red lipstick, etc.

LISTENING

Listening is often a more valued skill than speaking. Not only is it essential in the world of business, but listeners provide a fundamental sense of well being in all relationships. Listening is also overlooked as being important in acting. It's so easy to be burdened by memorizing lines, preparing emotionally, and remembering your blocking that listening just becomes the moment when you think ahead to your next line and your next move. Don't fall into that trap!

Hearing is not the same thing as listening. Most of us hear; few of us really listen. Listening isn't just about hearing. It's about reading body language and understanding what's being said in the silent moments.

Listening isn't as easy as it sounds. Most people are bad judges of their listening skills. Listening skills can weaken or strengthen any relationship. Think about the good listeners you have in your personal life. Those are more likely the people you connect with. Bad listeners don't typically make good companions.

"Noise" in communications is defined as interference in receiving a message. These interferences can be psychological, physiological, or external. Examples of these would be a character that is consumed with worry, a character that is ill, or a character that is paying attention to the radio. "Noise" can simply be an overload of information or other intrusive thoughts. All are distractions. So keep in mind what else is going on in the scene when your character is listening.

Regardless of interferences, listening still has its challenges. You will never fully understand every individual you meet. You can never be in that other person's mind. Your personal history and experiences are unique and color your perspective differently than anyone else. We all have our own individual view of the world around us. You may get the gist of what you are listening to, but you'll never see it *exactly* as it is meant coming from another person.

Decide if your character's listening skills are poor or good. Does your character:

- Pretend to listen when he is not?
- Just weed out the things he wants to hear and talks only about the things he cares to discuss?
- Listen, only to use the information that he gathers against others?
- Choose not to acknowledge certain unpleasantries?
- Take everything as an attack?

- Just want to tell his own stories, while ignoring the needs of others?

If you answered "yes" to any of those possibilities, then your character has some poor listening skills. The more you said "yes" to any of the above criteria, the more of a bad listener your character is. Does your character:

- Quietly and intently take in content?
- Ask questions along the way to show interest?
- Restate some of the issues at hand?
- Feel empathy for your speaker?
- Give supporting comments to your speaker?
- Dissect the problem?
- Appraise the situation?
- Offer some advice?

If you answered "yes" to any of the aforementioned criteria, you won't be surprised to learn that your character has some good listening skills. The more you answered "yes," the better of a listener your character is. Be attuned to these listening methods and it will help you to shape and understand more about your character.

RANDOM BITS

Take responsibility for your emotions, both as a human being and as an actor. You are largely in control of feeling the way you do in response to what is happening to you. (i.e. Do you get upset at a belated birthday card because someone forgot to send one on your actual date of birth, or are you appreciative that your special day was remembered after all?) You should know yourself and know how you react to certain situations. And certainly, when you are playing a character, you should know how he would react in response to his situation.

Communication is also largely influenced by back-story, time-periods, and cultural backgrounds of your character. Portraying a person from a different culture or from a different time period can be tricky. You must consider posture, dress, tone of voice, intonation, volume, and status. While much of what has been mentioned about communication is universal, its cultural context must be considered. For example, a smile is fairly universal for expressing happiness. The time and place for smiling is different in various cultures and may be inappropriate depending on the culture.

There are many factors to take into consideration when you are communicating, as your character. We have been communicating all of our lives, so it is easy to take these issues for granted. However, if you keep these factors in the front of your mind, your acting will certainly benefit.

A LITTLE HISTORY: TEACHERS AND METHODS

Be flexible with methods.

— Charlize Theron

Acting is not about being someone different. It's finding the similarity in what is apparently different, then finding myself in there."

— Meryl Streep

TEACHERS

While there have been many amazing acting teachers throughout the years, this book will briefly touch on the most renowned ones in recent times. These are the major names you will hear in certain circles of acting.

Perhaps the most highly regarded acting teacher in history is Russia's **Konstantin Sergeyevich Stanislavski** (1863-1938). His influence was and continues to be immeasurable. He was an actor, director, producer, coach, and the founder of the

Moscow Art Theatre, which opened in 1898. When you hear the phrase, "The Method," it is often referring to the system that Stanislavski actually created. Stanislavski's system urged actors to reach a "believable truth." Stanislavski asked actors to use their own memories, recall how they reacted to certain stimuli, and use this knowledge to express realistic emotions on stage. For instance, if an actor were to portray anger, he might think back to a personal incident where something made him furious. In his later years, Stanislavski relinquished his use of emotional memory claiming that it had negative side effects on the actor's mental well being and caused undesirable tension. Stanislavski later believed that the actor should have a full and complete understanding of the scripted circumstances to reach a truthful and believable emotional state.

Lee Strasberg (1901-1982) is often considered the official advocate of "The Method" technique that was invented by Stanislavski. Strasberg had studied in Moscow under Stanislavski early in his life and learned the basis of emotional memory from the creator himself. Strasberg's legacy lives on at The Lee Strasberg Theatre and Film Institute in New York City, where his teachings and philosophies continue to inspire students today.

Stella Adler (1901-1992) was an enormously influential as an acting teacher and studied under Stanislavski in 1934. Adler also gathered a wide array of acting experience from Broadway, Yiddish theater, and Hollywood. She also co-founded The Group Theatre with Strasberg and several other actors. The Group Theatre thrived for approximately ten years and included producers, actors, directors, and playwrights. Adler founded two schools that are still in operation today: Stella Adler Studio of Acting in New York City and

Stella Adler Academy of Acting and Theatre in Los Angeles.

Sanford (Sandy) Meisner (1905-1995) taught that "acting is the ability to live truthfully under imaginary circumstances." Although some actors believed his approach was unusual, it was effective and highly useful. The exercises his students focused on were in finding honesty and truth in the situations the actor is conveying.

Behind this technique lay the theory that the emotional truth should be produced from the character's situation, not simply from the actor's emotional playbook. In other words, do as your character would do and let the emotion be the byproduct of this action. This stems from the fact that all emotion is unique to each individual and to each specific situation.

Meisner also emphasized that an actor must have spontaneous reactions to his surroundings, as opposed to the dictates of Strasberg's method where emotion must come from the actor's memory. Meisner's emotion originates from imaginary events. His approach tends to re-sensitize your responses to the world, inspire creativity, and encourage you to get in touch with yourself. Meisner emphasizes "repetition exercises," emotional preparation, instinctive reactions, and truthfulness. In 1995, Meisner opened The Sanford Meisner Center for performing artists. Today, his methods are still widely used and appreciated.

METHODS

There are numerous "methods" that actors use to enrich their acting. Some actors play their characters on *and* off screen. A few of the actors rumored to have used this method include Daniel Day-Lewis, Jim Carrey, Angelina Jolie, and Christian Bale. However, taking this approach can certainly become a strain on an actor's personal life. The main idea behind this method is that the actor can fall more deeply into the typical thinking and behavior patterns of their character. Although this method is extreme, it can be very effective and beneficial when performance day comes.

Nicole Kidman exercises a lighter variation of the above-mentioned technique when perfecting her accent. If she is cast to play a character with a different accent than her own (she is Australian), she will adopt her character's accent full time in her personal life.

Another common method (or perhaps more common than you'd think) is one where the actor bases their character on the traits of a specific animal or combination of animals. Basically the character will remind the actor of a particular animal, and the actor will then study that animal more closely. Then the actor adopts some of the animal's traits, small movements, gestures, intonations, and facial expressions. It often leaves behind the essence or faint nuance of the animal without obnoxious mimicry. If done well, the audience will register the expressed trait, but won't necessarily know the animal it was based on or realize that it was based on an animal at all. Sir Anthony Hopkins used this technique when he played Hannibal Lecter. He based Hannibal on the combination of a crocodile and a tarantula. In hindsight, the resemblances of these particular animal traits are quite recognizable.

Different methods will work for different people. There isn't one sure technique that works for everyone. Don't ever feel that you need to use the same method with every character you portray. You may find the need to vary your technique choices as you take on vastly different characters throughout your career. Sometimes you can combine many methods of acting to acquire the greatest enrichment of character portrayal.

The technique that works best for me is truly being in the moment and reacting honestly to the circumstances. I add in animal traits or other methods as I see fit for the individual character. As you gain more experience, you will discover what works best for you. More approaches to refining characters and scenes are listed in the next section. More techniques for character development are listed in the Emotions and Conflict (page 95) and Character Development (page 111) sections of this book.

SECTION II: GETTING STARTED

REFINING MONLOGUES AND SCENES THROUGH EXERCISES

You know it's all right to be wrong, but it's not all right not to try.

— Sandy Meisner

To find layers and depth in your monologue or scene, try to perform with different approaches. For example, scream or whisper your lines. Inevitably you will find elements within your monologue or scene that you didn't see or feel before. Of course, you won't perform your final monologue by screaming the entire piece, but you may find a word or phrase that works better when it is said louder or with more authority. The exercises listed in this book are meant to spark creative ideas. Experimenting with new ways of approaching a role can breathe insight into who your character is and, as a result, you can make a stronger, fuller connection with your character. Each of the following exercises is designed to help you dig up more "goods" which, in turn, will give your monologue or scene more history, creativity, believability, and depth.

For more information on how to perform a monologue for an audition, please see the General Notes for Auditions section of this book.

MONOLOGUE EXERCISES

Do your *entire* monologue (or scene) like this:

- Say it as fast as you can.
- Say it as slow as you can.
- Scream your lines.
- Say it as quietly as you can.
- Be angry.
- Be nervous.
- Imagine you are running very late and about to miss your flight home.
- Do it while arranging items (such as chairs, cups, clothes). Once you find a satisfactory arrangement, change it.
- Go through a bag or your purse.
- Pace back and forth.
- Dance like a ballerina.
- Deliver it with a stutter.
- Act out the gestures but don't use any words.
- Imagine you are a pirate.
- Imagine you are a gangster.
- Imagine you are a gossipy hairdresser.
- Weep and sob throughout the whole piece.
- Eat like you're starving.
- Madly chew gum.
- Pause three seconds for every period and one second for every comma.
- Over-annunciate every word.
- Ignore all punctuation and italicized direction.
- Do it with no emotion.
- Do it with the opposite emotion than what your lines suggest.
- Do it as though you are talking to an infant.
- Stare at your focus point the entire time.

- Imagine you are ten years old; forty years old; eighty years old.
- Imagine you are extremely tall or short.
- Imagine you are outgoing, shy, elderly, or have ADD.
- Walk in a circle while doing your monologue.
- Use the whole length of the stage to pace back and forth.
- Change pace in your speech and/or mood; give the piece a variety of verbal and emotional texture.
- Focus on one object and don't take your eyes off of it.
- Do the whole piece in your own words.
- Do it as if you are fighting sleep.
- Do the whole piece as if you don't care at all about what you are saying.
- Do it as though you are trying to do the worst job you possibly can do.
- Do it as if you have to go to the bathroom.
- Do it as though you have a migraine.
- Do it over-the-top happy or do it as a "cheer."
- Do it with a stiff back.
- Do it with a limp.
- Do it while tap-dancing.
- Do it as though you are clinically depressed.
- Do it as though you've had too many cups of coffee.
- Do it as though you are drunk.
- "Walk and Talk": Walk around the room (or rooms) and read your monologue aloud, while concentrating on the text.
- "Walk and Talk": Walk around the room (or rooms) and read your monologue aloud, while

- absorbing the words your character is saying and why they are saying these things.
- Come up with an expression that summarizes your character's intention. It could be as simple as, "Not anymore" or as long as "Don't even think about touching me." Say the phrase after every sentence in your monologue. Then reduce the use of the expression by saying it several times, only at key moments. This helps put the focus back on the purpose behind everything your character is saying. Eventually you should take out the phrase you used and only the actual text remains. *Variation*: Do it with a physical gesture that symbolizes your character's state of mind.

MONOLOGUE EXERCISES WITH ANOTHER PERSON:

- Have another person repeat the same phrase to reinforce your character's state of mind. (i.e. – "You're worthless.")
- Have another person question each of your lines. Start with reading your first line only. Your partner will then say that first line back to you as a question. You will then answer the "question" your partner posed by stating that same line back to your partner. Then move on to the second line and so on. For example:
  PERSON A - I ran away as fast as I could.
  PERSON B - You ran away as fast as you could?
  PERSON A - I ran away as fast as I could.
  PERSON A - Reads the next line, etc.

When the actor answers the question with their line, there tends to be more honesty and conviction in their delivery.
- To improve concentration, have someone attempt to distract you as you perform.
- Improvise a scene based on the monologue.
- Read a sentence from the monologue, and have another person offer some advice on that sentence. They can also do a short improvisation on that line for a few moments before moving on to the next sentence. You can do this for several sentences or for the whole monologue.
- Tell your partner all about what has happened in the context of your monologue, and do it as your character. Use your own words. Your partner can ask you questions. When you are done, reflect on what you have found to be most important to your character.

SCENE AND DIALOGUE EXERCISES FOR ACTORS:

- Both actors should read through a new scene a few times. After they read the whole scene, they are to perform the scene without looking at the lines. This helps an actor gain confidence, explore characters, grasp dialogue, exercise logical choices, and bring characters to life.
- After reading an entire scene, both actors should continue to improvise *beyond* the end of the scene in order to explore their characters.
- Improvise a scene that takes place *before* your written scene. Again, this aids in character development and circumstantial exploration.

- Perform the scene in gibberish, but continue to keep the plot, gestures, and emotions. Only the words should be gobbledygook. This will help you to focus on everything outside of the actual text. Your gestures will likely be bigger.
- Perform the scene while each actor faces away from one another as an additional challenge to enhancing focus.
- Actors should face each other and perform the scene without emotion. This will force you to explore how much weight emotion carries within your scene. It will also bring attention to the more intense moments in the script.
- Have both actors circle one another like vultures throughout the scene. Note how this constant movement changes the scene.
- Trade characters with your acting partner. You will learn more, not only about your partner's character but about your character as well.
- Have an extra person distract the actors by getting in their way, making noises, asking questions, etc. throughout the entire scene. The two actors from the scene will do the best they can to ignore the "annoying person" as they perform the scene. This exercise should help enhance concentration skills.

MEMORIZATION

That is the basic need for art in life, not self-expression, but rather a saying and doing of things we cannot completely say or do in life but which have to be said and done.

— Lee Strasberg

Memorization is daunting to people who aren't accustomed to committing hundreds of lines to memory. Often times novice actors don't trust themselves to learn the lines of a script. But, once they jump in, they'll find that memorization comes easy to them. Here are several tips to memorization:

- Chunking – Memorize big bites at a time.
- Write it out – Create a mental picture of the lines in your own handwriting.
- Type it out – Clump lines into easy-to-remember sections. Use colors to symbolize mood.
- Recorder – Record lines and listen to them whenever possible.
- Wing it – Recite what lines you remember and see what you missed.
- Repetition – Read your lines over and over.
- Write out sentences or groups of sentences on index cards.

- Think about the ways that your topic relates to your life experiences and feelings.
- Review the sequence of ideas and dissect the progression of the piece. Really break down how one moment leads into the next.
- Equate word to memorable images.
- Practice the three R's – rehearse, rehearse, rehearse. Kinesthetic learning, or the act of "doing" your part over and over, will embed the words in your head. Sometimes the physical act of blocking on stage will help you to memorize your lines more easily, as well.
- Memorize your piece backwards. Place special attention on memorizing the last section of the piece. Often actors tend to focus most on the beginning.
- Implement acronyms.
- Memorize a word at a time and then slowly build the sentences together again: "I…I went…I went to…I went to the…I went to the market."

The use of a digital recorder allows actors to easily rehearse on their own. Record one segment with all of the actors' lines. Then record another segment omitting just your lines. Be sure to leave enough time for you to speak your lines. In the end you will have two segments to practice along with; one with your lines and one without.

Memorize your lines *plainly*. Don't attach any emphasis or emotion to the words you are learning. You should of course understand the meaning of what you say and the reason why it is said, but memorize the text robotically – almost like a list. This will help you to be more open and honest when you perform your piece. If you attach emotions to the process of memorizing your lines you will find it hinders your ability to react spontaneously and honestly when you are performing. Memorizing emotion along with the lines could force you to unnaturally emphasize certain words just because you always said it that way in practice. The emotion should not be *memorized* ahead of time. The emotion joins the scripted words *in the moment* and is played out honestly.

In the Emotions section of this book you will find several short scenes (on page 107). If you think you aren't capable of memorizing lines just yet, look over these pieces and choose a character. Be dedicated and take a few days to use any aforementioned technique(s) to memorize the lines. Use a digital recorder. Aim to perform the whole scene without looking at your lines. Don't give up. You'll surprise yourself!

GENERAL NOTES FOR AUDITIONS

Actors tend to get in their own way, a lot. A lot of times you will do things that will screw up your auditioning process. I was very bad at auditioning, and I always went in to it saying 'God I hope I don't screw this up.' But at the same time, the directors are saying, 'God, I hope this person is the savior.' You have to remember that the worst thing that could happen is you don't get the job you don't already have.

— George Clooney

You cannot research enough.

— Brad Pitt

Be Professional, Reliable, and Prepared

      The three greatest tips for being a part of any performance are to be professional, reliable, and prepared. If you possess these three qualities, there will be no mistake about your dedication and you will maintain a fine reputation. Think of an audition as a job interview. Whether you are being paid or not, technically you are applying for a job. Keep in mind that you want to make a good impression and show off your skills.

Finding Auditions

Where can you find auditions? With the Internet, audition postings are easier to find now than ever before. Any search engine (such as Google, Yahoo, or Bing) will help you to find a neighboring community theatre, film office, or reputable agency near you. If you reach out to them, they will likely put you on their contact list for auditions and newsletters. Get to know one of the greatest United States auditions services: Backstage.com. Backstage can give you some excellent leads if you live close to a big city. Also check out the Arts section of your local newspaper once a week for audition postings. Some Facebook pages or Craigslist.org ads can open some doors to legitimate auditions, but always be wary and do your research when you are dealing with questionable sources.

Monologues

Auditions may ask for a prepared monologue, so have a few monologues of varying genres already prepared. I suggest having three age and gender appropriate monologues memorized: one dramatic, one seriocomic, and one comical. Know what type of film or show you're auditioning for and come prepared with an appropriately themed monologue.

If you are interested in auditioning for staged productions in addition to film and TV, prepare monologues from published plays. Most theatre companies simply prefer monologues from plays. Sometimes they specifically ask for a "classic" piece or something from Shakespeare. Plays are written to be performed on the stage so that is, in itself, an advantage to auditioning for a theatre. Material from plays also tends to lend itself well to auditioning for film and TV, making it more universal.

    Beware of picking a monologue that is from a film you know all too well. If you are too familiar with another actor's performance, you may find yourself inadvertently copying the actor's performance. This completely takes away from the honest, individual approach you would offer the role. In a way, it contaminates your performance. Try to find an unfamiliar monologue, something that connects deeply with you and ignites a little fire in your heart.

    Your monologue should run between one and a half to two minutes. Most audition postings will indicate a time frame for the monologues, but just less than two minutes seems to be a common standard. For children, the standard is even shorter, ranging from forty-five to sixty seconds in length.

    You can find monologues almost anywhere on the Internet, but monologue books are an excellent resource as well. Many monologue books are organized in a way where you can easily navigate through genre, age, gender, and other various factors. Some books are built around specific genres or genders alone, which can instantly narrow down your search even more. You can also borrow or purchase specific scripts. If you can, obtain a script of the show you are auditioning for. If you can read the script, become familiar with the content, and narrow down what characters you are capable of playing, it will certainly work to your advantage.

Keep in mind that a monologue will be performed in a slightly different manner as a solo piece, than it will as presented within the show itself. You will want to consider exhibiting some of your dramatic range when you audition with a monologue, whereas, in a show you'll have the entire script to play out your character's journey. So, if you choose to show a bit of range, you want to be sure your monologue isn't too bland or stagnant. Present more than one basic emotion. We all feel more than just one singular emotion at a time. So figure out which emotions your character has within them and be sure they all surface in one way or another. Most monologues either begin with one extreme emotion and end in the opposite extreme, or they are layered with emotional texture. Use intonation, pace, volume, physical gesture, posture, purposeful motion, and character choices to really give your performance gusto. But remember to always be sure all of your choices are rooted in truth.

You should always know as much about your character and their circumstance before you perform the monologue. Anything outside of the details you are given will need to be made up through your imagination. You want to give an informed performance. Know where you are, who you are talking to, and what has caused your character to say these lines. Also be sure to know exactly where the person is that you are addressing. This will be your "focus spot." Pick a sign, a window, or some other location (usually around eye-level) and focus on that location consistently as you address the person. If you are in front of a camera, you might want to pick a focus spot around the lens, but not directly into the lens. Never use another person or a camera as a focus spot, unless you are directed to do so.

Prop Use and Apparel

Props are wonderful tools that can enhance scenes and monologues, but during auditions props can be cumbersome and distracting. Most professionals in the acting industry warn against using props during auditions. The use of a prop should be rehearsed. If you are reading from a script, a prop will only get in the way. If you want to use a prop for a prepared monologue, it should be a small, simple item. In most instances items that you already have on you are often acceptable like tissues, glasses, or a mobile phone. If you are thinking of bringing in something like a megaphone and pom-poms, you might want to rethink your choice. Pantomime is a better alternative for large, distracting props. Use careful judgment when deciding whether to incorporate a prop into an audition.

Also keep in mind the type of clothing you wear to an audition. Depending on the time period and the character you are auditioning for, you want to wear appropriate attire. Dress more lavishly for a royal role and dress more casually for the role of a beggar on the street, but don't feel the need to dress in the extreme. Some actors "go all out" and dress exactly as their character would dress. Sometimes that works, but sometimes it backfires because it takes the focus away from your performance. The bottom line is to do what makes you feel the most confident and comfortable.

Cold Readings

Most audition calls ask for a cold reading of some sort. This usually means that some sides (dialogue or text from the play or show) are made available to the auditioning actors at the audition. The actors then have some time before their audition to read over these lines before reading them "cold" in front of their auditors. Sometimes the actor will be asked to stay to read again for a different character, or they may be dismissed for that day and contacted at a later time to return for a "call back." A call back is a second or subsequent audition for actors as the auditors narrow down the pool of potential actors for their production.

When you prepare to audition for a cold read scene, you'll need to break down the material. Sometimes you'll have ample time to familiarize yourself with the scene and sometimes you'll have to speed up the process to only a few minutes. Read it over a few times to really understand the content. Then try to answer the following questions:

- **What triggered the scene?** Think about what must have taken place prior to the scene to cause it to happen. This will help you to get into the right state of mind as well as set the tone for the scene before it starts.
- **Learn more about the character.** You can do this through nuggets of information in the script and inferences from the text. The character description, information given about the scene, and clues from the dialogue exchange are all excellent sources for figuring out more about who your character is and what his objectives are.
- **What is the genre?** Is it a comedy? Is it a tragic drama? The tone of the show should probably weigh in on your performance and character choices.
- **Summarize the plot.** What is it that your character wants? What is he going to do to get it? What complications are in his way? What happened up to this point that has caused the

crisis? Are all of these things building up to a climactic point? What will your character do if he gets what he wants?
- **Where are you?** You have to have a fairly clear idea of where you are during the scene.
- **Who are you talking to and where are they?** If you are acting in a scene with one or two other actors, you'll obviously interact with them. But if you're also addressing a crowd that isn't there, you need to know where that crowd is located.

How Auditions Are Set Up

Every audition is orchestrated in a different way. Most auditions either assign time slots for each actor, or they have a sign-in sheet at the audition on a first-come, first-served basis. If it is a big budget production, you may experience a "cattle call," where you stand in a lengthy line for hours on end to be given a group lecture, leaving behind your headshot and resume (and often never speaking directly to anyone involved in casting). And there are various other types of auditions thanks to modern technology. You can now send your reel to someone in casting, use YouTube to download an audition, or audition live via Skype.

Even with the miraculous advancements in technology, auditioning in person is still most common. This is the best way the audition panel can really "feel" your performance and get a decent idea of who you are as a person.

The audition itself can take place almost anywhere: an office, a stage, a random room, someone's house, or a rented conference room. I know of auditions being held in hallways or outside on a stage before an audience on live TV. Some auditions allow everyone auditioning to watch each performance. Other auditions are private, with each actor being called in one by one. Sometimes you'll be excused immediately after your audition, or sometimes you might be asked to stay a little longer. When you are asked to stay after your initial audition, it's usually because they want you to read with another actor *or* to read for a different character. More often than not, if you are being considered for a role, you are asked to attend a "call back" audition at a later time.

Who Are the Auditors?

Generally speaking there are at least one, and as many as five or more people, sitting in on any given audition. Auditors are generally the artistic director, a casting director, other pre-cast actors, board members, investors, or anyone related to the core of the production. They ultimately are relying on you for your talent in their production.

Here is some advice for auditioning. The first list of general tips should be applied to both monologue and cold read auditions:

Quick General Tips for any Audition:

1. Share a *firm* handshake with your auditors.

2. Keep an upright, positive posture (but remember to use the appropriate posture of your character when you are acting).

3. Be emotionally prepared. If you can fill yourself with the proper emotion to start off the monologue or cold read, it will serve your entire piece much better. You should always begin your scene in the appropriate state of mind. You can do this through

imagination, a memory, a photograph, or a song. Whichever you choose, it should trigger a similar emotion to the one your character is experiencing.

4. Keep a positive, confident mood. Be helpful, cooperative, and energetic. Be the best "you" that you can be and show how professional you are.

5. If possible, read any lines they give you before you go into the audition. Do not feel you need to memorize the lines, unless requested to.

6. When you "slate" with your name at the start of your audition, keep it simple and confident. Usually you are only asked to state your name and the title of the piece you are going to perform. Treat that moment as professionally as possible. Don't use that time to preface anything about your performance, if the auditors have any questions, they'll certainly ask.

7. Whenever possible, look up from your paper. The auditors want to see your face.

8. Project your voice. Also be sure that your posture, breathing, volume, and enunciation are contributing to the manner in which your character speaks.

9. Do not follow lines with your finger. Instead, use your finger as a "marker," to help you find where you left off.

10. Highlighter your lines (if allowed).

11. Never look directly into the camera or at the auditors, unless directed to do so. If you are alone and delivering a monologue to someone, pick a spot

where this imaginary person is and commit to that "focus spot" for the duration of your monologue.

12. Give a moment or a few seconds after your performance to break free of character, and then thank the auditors for the audition.

13. If the auditors ask if you have any questions, ask them when casting will be complete.

14. Always thank the audition panel for their time.

Quick Monologue Tips for Auditions:

1. Don't look at the floor. This makes you look lost, confused, and unprepared. Only look down if the stage directions tell you to do so. Otherwise, make an effort to look up. The more the auditors see of your face and eyes, the better.

2. Be in love with your monologue. If you're doing a piece that you hate or are tired of, it's time to switch it up and find something new. If you aren't satisfied with your monologue, it will come through in your performance.

3. Don't fidget. Take control of your actions and make them work for your character. Keep your motions purposeful.

4. Keep a happy, positive disposition when entering and exiting an audition space. While the auditors are interested in your skills, they also are interested in discovering who you are as a person. A cheery, friendly, and upbeat attitude will always triumph over a less outgoing one.

5. Be aware of how your voice is projecting, and make sure that you aren't mumbling. Know your space. Be sure that you annunciate and fill up the room with the proper volume.

6. Steer clear of accents, unless you are specifically directed to do so.

7. Identify your staging area and perform in that space accordingly. Don't stand too close to auditors and invade their space.

8. Have your lines memorized. Repeat them to the point where they are second nature. You can't memorize them enough.

9. Do your best to let the language of the piece become a part of you. It's best to know every word and pause appropriately, in any given piece. Paraphrasing will work in emergencies (if you have forgotten your lines), but it's a last resort.

10. Use your space to your advantage. Standing in one position can make your performance stagnant. Open yourself up and physically express yourself. Imagine how you'd like to see someone else present this piece and give it the same energy.

11. Face forward! Perform for your auditors. Don't look directly at them, but understand that they need to get the full experience of your audition. Find a focal point, just off to the side or behind the auditors, and stick with that choice for the whole monologue.

12. Define your character's objective and play out the actions to achieve that goal. Recognize what is important to the character. Understand where your

character comes from and what he wants to accomplish.

Quick Cold Read Tips for Auditions:

1. A beneficial exercise you can do, in advance of a cold read audition, is to regularly practice reading things that are unfamiliar to you. Pick up a script, book, or any article and start reading it *out loud*. The practice of reading "cold" material out loud will certainly strengthen your skills.

2. Research is always a helpful practice in preparation of a cold read audition. If you are auditioning for a play, and can obtain a copy of the script, then read the play. Have an idea of what characters you can audition for. If you can't obtain a copy of the script, base your research from the information provided in the character's description. For example, if the character you are auditioning for is a veterinarian who was recently diagnosed with diabetes, you can research that character's occupation and disorder to gain insight. The more information you can gather about the play or character you are auditioning for, the more it will benefit you.

3. Familiarize, don't memorize. As soon as you get the sides, read over them as often as you can. Never feel the need to memorize anything unless you can easily do so, or if you are specifically asked to memorize it.

4. Analyze the scene. Figure out the basics: who are you, who are you talking to, where are you, and what do you want? Know what you are talking

about. Understand what your character is saying and doing and why they're saying and doing it.

5. Relax, breathe, and be sure you pace yourself. When you are sitting in the waiting room before your audition, try to go over your material in a relaxed state of mind. Focus on slowing down your breathing, if it helps. When you begin your audition, make sure your pace is appropriate and not rushed, due to your nerves.

6. Be sure to move. Use the space that you are given to express yourself. Being still can be very stagnant and boring. Be engaged in your character and situation and fill up your space. Of course, be sure the physicality is effective in serving the character and their circumstance.

7. Make sure you are listening. If you are fully engaged in the scene, this should come naturally. Listening to the other characters in the scene is often what gives you the impetus to do or say what comes next. During moments where you aren't speaking and don't need to be looking at the script, be sure to listen and react to everything around you.

8. Be open to re-reading the script. Sometimes the audition panel will ask you to read the sides again in a different way than you originally read. Don't feel offended if they do this. It could mean that they have you in mind for a different character, or maybe they want to see how well you take direction. Maybe they want to test your range as an actor. Sometimes they want to see a variety in the character. Whatever the reason may be, really listen to any direction that is given and use this newfound opportunity to show off your talent.

9. Get creative. If you can tell the character is angry, your first inclination may be to raise your voice. But think about how a calm, quiet, barely contained anger could effectively contribute to the character even more. Don't always go for the obvious. Remember that there are numerous ways of showing an emotion. Develop a unique character with honesty and an open mind. Never sacrifice a believable performance for the sake of making a memorable impression. If you can, try to give a great performance with a creative character.

Headshots

Headshots are a great tool for any actor and in many instances a requirement. A headshot is a professional photo accurately depicting an actor's face at its best. Make sure the photo looks like "you." Headshots are not meant to be glamour shots. Wrinkles, moles, and other permanent facial features should not be touched up in your picture. A headshot basically needs to reflect what you will look like to the audition panel when you enter. If you look too young, too old, or too unpolished compared to your photo, auditors may develop a negative feeling about you.

The photo should frame your face from your shoulders and up. Choose a natural pose and facial expression. Don't force a smile if it isn't "you." Steer away from posing "over the shoulder" or putting your hands into the frame of the shot. Face forward and look directly into the camera. If you wear glasses or have facial hair, you can choose to do headshots with and without those features. But, in the end, you always want to have one standard headshot that you submit to casting calls.

The background of the headshot should not take attention away from your face. Be sure the background isn't too trendy in the way that it could easily "date" your picture. Also make sure your face isn't half hidden in shadows; it is important that all of your features are clearly depicted. Keep the background neutral and make sure the lighting is appropriate.

Pick something simple, solid, plain, and professional to wear. Any clothing with overly bright colors or patterns will compete for attention with your face. Choose solid colored tops that are flattering and professional looking.

Once upon a time, black and white headshots were more desirable than colored photos. The trend has now changed, especially on the west coast of the United States. Black and white might still be used in rare instances, but colored headshots are now the norm.

Headshots are usually eight by ten inches. The name of the actor should be printed across the bottom of the photo, and sometimes a resume is printed on the back.

When auditioning for professional theatre, film, or television shows, you will likely need a headshot for serious consideration. When submitting for films and television, a three-quarter body shot is sometimes requested as well. However, most of the time, three-quarter and full-body shots are used for modeling, not acting. For most community theatres you can often audition without a photo or professional headshot, thanks to digital photography.

You don't have to invest much money in getting a decent headshot anymore. If you're just starting out, have a friend take your headshot at an interesting location that offers a neutral, complimentary background. You can turn those photos into professional looking headshots on your computer. There are also companies such as Abcpictures.com and

Reproductions.com that mass-produce headshots for reasonable prices.

If you are serious about pursuing acting as a career, research photographers and have your headshots done professionally once you have a decent resume to couple with it.

Resume Content and Formatting

Resumes are not always required at auditions. Many auditions have a sheet (much like a job application), which actors fill out upon arrival. This sheet generally asks for your contact information as well as a space to list experience. If you don't have experience, you can list related experiences you've had such as public speaking. Don't lie. Be honest about your acting experiences. Casting directors are typically looking for talent, type, and dependability above anything else.

A resume and CV (curriculum vitae) are slightly different from one another and vary in look, length, and content. A resume is a bit more concise and ranges from one to two pages, where a CV is a bit more detailed and may be longer. Resumes are typically preferred over CV's when it comes to acting. Generally, a performing arts resume would include all of your recent and relevant experience in theater, film, television, and commercial work. This includes related arts such as voiceover experience. Also include your degrees, specialty classes, awards, and honors. The best way to organize all of your experience will depend on your individual circumstance. There are plenty of resume examples available online when you type "acting resume samples" into a search engine.

Formatting your acting resume is simple. At the top of the page you can generally include: your name, affiliation (union, non-union), address, e-mail address, phone number, height, weight, eye color, and hair color. Next, you should list any experience you have in theatre, film, television, and commercials. List the project name, character name/title, and production company for each experience you want to include on your resume.

If you have any training in performing arts, you should list the coach's name, class, and location. At the end of your resume you can add a section for "special skills." List any unique talents that may be relevant or give you some edge. Examples of these are: foreign language skills, martial arts, singing, or dance training.

Beware of Scams

If you are required to pay an "agency" for their services, then beware. A legitimate agent won't ask for money. An agent should find work for you and make money when you land and complete a paying job. The percentage they take can range from ten to twenty percent. Actors in the union typically pay ten percent, and non-union actors usually pay twenty percent.

The best way to find a reputable agency is through thorough research. Ask around at local theatres or look for blogs that discuss agency reputations. Additionally, if you have the time, ask for an interview with the agency to get a better idea of how they operate. Some agencies also make money through offering classes, workshops, headshots, and other services. Investigate these services a little further to find out how much they are worth investing your time and money. Some great agencies can offer mediocre services for the prices they charge. Careful research is always a good idea. Additionally, some reputable agencies will often ask you for a monthly fee to include you in their web site database. You can judge for yourself if the payments are worthwhile.

Always be wary of anyone promising jobs, money, or fame. The best way to find a legitimate agency or gig is to go through word-of-mouth and background checks. That also goes for any audition. Some organizations are poorly organized and productions can fall through very easily. Unfortunately there are plenty of agencies or casting calls that feed off of people who are hungry for fame and fortune. Your best bet is to be cautious, ask questions, and do your research.

Dealing with Rejection

I take rejection as someone blowing a bugle in my ear to wake me up and [get me] going, rather than retreat.

— Sylvester Stallone

The product you're selling is you. So when they say they don't want you, they say they don't want you personally...and it hurts. And it costs you something every time.

— George Clooney

No one likes rejection. Everyone wants to be successful. It's only natural. But when you get into the acting world, you have to understand that it is rife with rejection. Being cast in a lead role wouldn't be nearly as rewarding if you could simply walk into an audition and ask for it. Learn to embrace rejection and let it go.

Sometimes the competition is overwhelming and your chances of being cast are slim, simply due to that. Perhaps your lack in experience may hold you back. Sometimes the talent is there but you're physically too tall, too short, too young, or too old compared to someone else. Maybe you're just right, but a different actor is better matched up with the actress who has already been cast. No one person is suited for every role. Most of the time, you won't know why you weren't cast. Oftentimes you won't know for certain that you were rejected, because most casting directors don't have the time or the staff to make those kinds of callbacks.

Casting is largely determined by type. Talent also carries a lot of weight in the casting process. Your personality is also taken into consideration. If all things are judged equally in type and talent, the person who will get cast will likely be the one who is most desirable to work with. What makes you desirable to work with? Having a kind, helpful, and polite personality, and showing how professional you are by arriving on time and being prepared. But even if you have all three key elements: type, talent, and personality – your chances may be very slight depending on how thick the competition is.

As an actor, you have to remember that you aren't made to play every role. You are unique. Uniqueness and individuality is a good thing - because there are some roles that you are made for that most other actors are not.

The best advice is to expect nothing. That is much easier said than done, but it will save you emotional wear and tear. If you keep yourself busy and audition for several roles at a time, you will eventually get your foot in the door somewhere.

Every experience is all about networking. As you meet other people in the industry, the acting world will begin to open up to you. Many places also seek volunteers for behind-the-scenes work. You could volunteer for any one of these jobs: costumes, props, scenery, location scouting, ushering, etc. This type of opportunity also helps to get your foot in the door. Use it to your advantage and show how dependable and dedicated you are. As an added bonus, you'll gain much from the other actors and learn firsthand how productions are staged.

After each audition, no matter how you feel you did, give yourself some "bravery credits." Chalk it off as a learning experience. The more you audition in front of auditors, the better you will become with auditioning.

Rejection isn't necessarily "no" forever; it's only "no" for now. If you think of it this way, it brings you a degree of comfort. I can't tell you how many times I was initially told "no" and the same people came back to me at a later time and offered me a chance to work on a different project. Whenever you meet people at an audition, you are networking. And if you make a positive impression, you are *remembered*. So even if you weren't right for the role they were casting for on the day you first met, you might stick out in an auditor's mind for a different role in the future.

Failure is bittersweet. Of course, rejection is not a great feeling and even knowing that the rejection is probably based on things beyond your control doesn't bring much comfort either. But rejection does have some positive elements: a lesson learned, another experience, one more step in the right direction, another bridge built, more connections made, motivation in disguise. Rejection has the unique power to both break you down *and* build you up.

Don't get discouraged by rejection. If you have the acting bug, the best way to feed it is to keep practicing and auditioning. And it never hurts to take more acting classes to keep things fresh.

PERFORMANCE EVALUATIONS

Life beats down and crushes the soul and art reminds you that you have one.

— Stella Adler

Many actors are their most brutal critic. But if you think you can evaluate yourself fairly, then set up a video camera and record your performance. This will get you out of your head. When you view the video you'll find that sometimes you'll be spot-on, but other times, what you intended to express isn't coming through in your performance.

If you have a performance on video, it may be best to set it aside and not watch it for some time, possibly a week or longer. If a performance is too fresh in your head, you can't judge it fairly.

If you hear a little voice in your head judging yourself as you are performing, quiet it. First of all, it is nearly impossible to judge yourself as you are acting. Secondly, if you are judging yourself, you aren't as invested in your character as you ought to be. Always be doing and thinking as your character would.

Remember that what feels "off" or wrong may work well for your character and what feels good or correct may not work. It may not feel good to get a shot or immunization, but it is ultimately for your greater good. It may feel good to find a stranger's misplaced wallet stuffed with hundred dollar bills, but it isn't necessarily a good thing to keep it for yourself. The bottom line is – what feels right may be wrong, and what feels bad may be good. An example of this could be the director telling you to lean over the edge of the sofa more obviously and intently in order to eavesdrop on a conversation in the other room. Maybe leaning over any further feels overly dramatic and uncomfortable to you. But the director might tell you that it's perfect and looks much better that way. Now you have to find a way to make that new direction purposeful to your character. The same could be said for a character choice. When I chose a monologue with a ditzy character, I played her part-ditz. I didn't want her to be too much of a caricature because I still wanted the character to be believable. After performing the piece in several different ways for some colleagues of mine, they all agreed that part-ditz was decent, but full-ditz worked much better. At first this choice seemed too forced to me. But after considering it, I realized I simply had to change some things about the way I perceived the character to make full-ditz work.

      The best remedy is to get feedback from an unbiased audience who can honestly tell you what is working and what is not. This is a huge reason why taking acting classes can mold your craft more effectively. The evaluations you will receive from your peers and instructors are a good tool to gauge your performance and portrayal of a character. If you evaluate yourself in addition to that, compare your notes with your peers. All evaluations need to be considered, whether you receive positive or negative advice. Even the least informed critique can offer a useful suggestion and fresh perspective. Before rejecting any feedback, no matter how irrelevant it may seem, put it aside and read it later. Often, on a second glance, you may fund a nugget of truth to improve your performance. The forms below offer guidelines and criteria that can fine-tune your performance.

PERFORMANCE EVALUATION & CHECKLIST:

PREPARATION
_ Do you have everything memorized?
_ Did you research thoroughly?
_ Did you have adequate rehearsals?

INTERPRETATION
_ Does your characterization reflect the author's intent?
_ Is your characterization believable, honest, and natural?
_ Are your character's objectives clear?
_ Do you project the appropriate emotional tone?
_ Do your choices reflect the time period accurately?
_ Do your choices reflect properly on the culture?

VOCAL
_ Does the vocal quality fit your character?
_ Are you projecting appropriately?
_ Does the pitch and inflection work with the character?
_ Do you use a variety of intonation in your voice?
_ Are you clear with your diction and articulation?
_ Is the dialect or accent consistent and correct throughout?

PACE
_ Does your pacing suit the character and the situation?
_ Is your pace energetic enough?

PHYSICALITY
_ Do physical movements reflect the personality of the character?
_ Do physical movements reflect the attitudes of the

character?
- Do you have consistent physical presence?
- Do you use appropriate facial expressions?
- Are your gestures expressing the character traits?
- Is your body language expressing the character traits?
- Are your physical conditions depicted properly through movement and posture?

CONCENTRATION
- Do you remain in character at all times?
- Does your character listen and respond accurately?
- Are you certain that you don't break the "fourth wall"?
- Do you pay attention to the specifics of your character?
- Do you over-generalize your character?
- Are you believable in your character?
- Are you on top of your cues?

OVERALL STORY
- Have you fully considered the full arch of the story?
- Have you thoroughly dealt with all conflict?

BLOCKING
- Do you execute your blocking accurately and on cue?
- Are you using the blocking to enhance the meaning of the scene?
- Are you being inventive with the blocking?
- Do you remain open to the audience?

OTHER
- Are you using your props to the characters advantage?
- Do you use your costume to its potential?
- Do you use the set to its full potential?
- Are your on-stage interactions working and connecting for the overall story?

SELF-EVALUATION

Name: _____

Performance Piece: _____

If I could perform this piece again, **I would like to change** _____
_____
_____
_____

I would **try** _____
_____
_____
_____

I believe the **best parts** of my performance were _____
_____
_____

My reasons are _____
_____
_____
_____

The parts of my performance **lacking** were _____
_____
_____
_____

My reasons are _____
_____
_____
_____

The **three most important things** I have learned from this piece are_____
_____
_____
_____

I feel my performance of this piece **exceeded / met / approached** my expectations.

PEER EVALUATION

Name of Performer:_____

EX- Excellent   **VG-** Very Good   **G-** Good   **F-** Fair

BELIEVABILITY
Is the actor honest and behaving truthfully in their interpretation?
   EX - VG - G - F

CONSISTENCY
Does the actor stay in character?
   EX - VG - G - F

MEMORIZATION
Are all lines fully memorized?
   EX - VG - G - F

PROJECTION
With both voice and personality?
   EX - VG - G - F

PACE
Is the timing and rate of speech appropriate?
   EX - VG - G - F

VOCAL SKILLS
What is the quality of the actor's accents and voice?
   EX - VG - G - F

ENGAGING
Is the actor's performance alluring?
EX - VG - G - F

ENERGETIC
Is it appropriately enthusiastic?
EX - VG - G - F

PHYSICAL SKILLS
How well does the actor move and use his body?
EX - VG - G - F

TEAM WORK
Does the cast work together?
EX - VG - G - F - N/A

IMPROVEMENT
Did the performance improve the second time?
EX - VG - G - F - N/A

What did you **enjoy** about this performance?

_____
_____
_____
_____
_____

What could use **improvement**?

_____
_____
_____
_____
_____

SECTION III: ELEMENTS OF ACTING

WARM UPS & GAMES

This section will steer actors through the fundamentals of exploring characters, emotions, listening skills, improvisation, and more. All of the topics discussed are related to each other very closely.

The warm-ups are usually used with small groups or in class settings, but some of them can be tailored for use with only one or two people.

Here you will find games that have been used in my classes and are loved dearly by my students. Nearly all of these games are rooted in improvisation. Every exercise listed is useful in improving all aspects of performance. However, each game and exercise targets specific skills. You will find this key helpful in determining which warm ups and games will be beneficial to you.

INT/WU - Introductions/Warm-Up (Icebreakers)
EMO - Emotions
CD - Character Development
GTY - Get in Touch with Yourself
LIS - Listening
FREIMG - Freeing Your Imagination & Creativity
USPC - Using Space
IMPROV - Improvisation
CONC - Concentration

ABC GAME [CONC; LIS] - All players sit in a circle. As a group, everyone decides on a topic (ex. food, animals, etc.). The first player says a word that starts with an "A." The person to their right says the "A" word and assigns a word for "B." The third person then repeats the "A" and "B" words and then assigns a word for "C," and so on. The object is to get to "Z" without anyone messing up. *Variation*: Substitute numbers for letters. One cantaloupe, two pears, three bananas, four guavas, five limes, etc.

ABC SCENARIOS [CONC; LIS] - Two actors decide on a relationship and a scenario and then play out the scene starting each sentence with the next letter of the alphabet. You can start with the letter "A" or you can begin anywhere in the alphabet. Example: **H**ow does it taste? **I**t tastes sweet. **J**ust leave a bite for me. '**K**, I will. **L**et me see it.

ALPHABET THROW [INT/WU; CONC] - Here's a great game for sharpening concentration and getting in-synch with a group of people. The group sits in a circle. The first person says "A" and points to another person in the circle. This person in turn says "B" and points to another person who says "C," and so on. The object is to see how fast you can get through the alphabet. *Variation:* You can also try this with numbers. For an added challenge, time the group on each round and try to beat your record.

ASSASSIN AND BODYGUARD [INT/WU; USPC] - This is a fabulous warm up game for a group of seven or more people. Each person secretly selects someone to be their "assassin" and another person to be their "bodyguard." These identities must be kept secret.

When the game begins, everyone tries to stay away from their assassin by staying near or behind the protection of their bodyguard. After a few minutes each person tries to guess who was picked for which role.

BING BONG BANG **[CONC; LIS; IMPROV]** - Four actors enter the playing space. Actors #1, #2, and #3 face away from the audience and cover their ears. The audience suggests to actor #4 a simple idea such as: sneezing, hiccupping, laughter, blowing your nose, sleeping through a thunderstorm, seeing a ghost, etc. Actor #4 now communicates this expression to actor #1 through mime and gibberish while the other two actors remain facing away with their ears covered. Then actor #1 tries to communicate the gesture to #2, and finally #2 to #3. At the end, all players must describe the idea correctly.

COMMANDEER **[LIS; CONC; IMPROV]** - Four actors are needed for this game. One actor plays the hijacker and leaves the playing space. The other three actors decide on a means of transportation to the crime scene, a weapon (which can be silly like a spoon or a beach ball), and a goal for the hijacker (the object he steals). When the hijacker returns to the scene, the other actors (who typically play the victims in the scene) must act out their roles and give hints to the hijacker. He must determine the mode of transportation, the weapon, and his goal in order to finish the game.

COMMON OBJECT **[CD; LIS; IMPROV]** - An object is placed on a single chair on stage. Three predetermined actors take turns performing a monologue incorporating the object. The first actor does a short monologue about that object. He may use the object as a prop, but must replace it by the end of the monologue for the next actor. The second actor builds on his predecessor's monologue incorporating the object and his predecessor's character. The third must incorporate both of the previous monologues and build a connection to the other two actors' characters. The object is to connect with the other actors and build a story. Try not to be overly predictable with the choices.

CONFESS **[LIS; CONC; IMPROV]** - This game takes two players: an interrogator and a suspect. The suspect leaves the playing space while the group chooses three items or actions for the suspect's crime. After the suspect returns, the scene starts. The suspect must figure out the three items from his interrogator's accusations. The suspect must confess to using the object(s) or doing the action(s) to end the game.

COPY CAT WALK **[CONC; USPC]** - All actors stand in a line. The first actor begins to walk *normally*. After a few moments, the second actor follows the first one, making every effort to move just like the first actor. The first actor then goes to the back of the line. The second actor then walks in his own normal way, and the third actor follows the second actor, and so on.

FOREIGN FILM **[IMPROV; FREIMG]** - Two actors play out a scene in gibberish, two other actors translate what the two gibberish actors are "saying."

GIBBERISH MASTER **[FREIMG; IMPROV]** - An actor gives a speech in gibberish on "how to do something." Another actor on stage translates his speech as he speaks. *Variation*: The actor tells a story, or recites a poem in gibberish. Be sure that the translation is the same number of lines, beats, and rhyme as the gibberish poem.

GIBBERISH REPEAT **[CD; LIS]** - Two actors play out a short scene and then do it again speaking in bibberish.

GREETINGS AND SALUTATIONS **[INT/WU; EMO; CD]** - Actors pair up and greet one another. Each actor *silently* greets the other using only movements and gestures. The rest of the group must try to guess the pair's relationship. Each pair should select from the following list:

- long lost friends
- someone with horrible breath
- someone you don't trust
- an ex-boyfriend or ex-girlfriend
- your favorite sibling
- someone you detest
- your next door neighbor you dislike
- a job applicant you're about to interview
- someone you have a secret crush on
- an acquaintance who works in your building
- your boss
- someone you just rear-ended in traffic
- your child's teacher
- someone who sold you a flawed used car
- the person behind the counter at the bakery
- your old elementary school teacher

HEARING VOICES **[IMPROV; FREIMG; CD]** - One actor plays in this scene. Other actors stand off to the side and give voices to the objects in the scene. Example: the actor is browsing in a bakery and a cream puff talks. Any object can have a voice, as long as it is made immediately clear *what* is speaking either through the actor's movements or the voices.

HIDDEN QUALITIES [CD; LIS] – Give four actors characteristics such as greedy, prissy, snobby, etc. on a slip of paper. One actor plays the interviewer and must ask the other actors questions. The other actors must respond and demonstrate their characteristic. At the end of the scene, the group must guess every actor's secret quality.

HITCHHIKER [EMO; CD] – Assign each actor an emotion (or they can choose one). The first person plays the driver and he picks up his passengers one by one. As each person enters the vehicle they must creatively convey their specific emotion or attribute. It could be sadness or excitement coming from a child, or someone with a stutter. When the trait becomes clear to the others in the vehicle, all of the passengers must adopt that emotion. Each passenger should be allowed fifteen to thirty seconds before the next passenger enters. *Variation*: For fun, this exercise can be done in different accents.

INSTA-STORY [FREIMG; LIS] - This exercise illustrates how easy it is to develop an original story. Divide all actors in half and have Group One leave the room. Tell Group One that Group Two has come up with a great story and it is their job to guess the plot. But they are only allowed to ask yes or no questions. Tell Group Two that they must answer these questions based on the following rules: any question asked that beginning with a vowel will be answered with a "no." If they answer with "no" twice in a row, they must answer the next question with a "yes". After Group Two understands the game, bring Group One back in and pair a member from each group together. Each pair will come up with their own story. Let the game continue until someone catches on.

IN CONCLUSION **[IMPROV; FREIMG]** – Give a line to a pair of actors. The actors must then play out a scene ending with the supplied line. *Variation*: The given line is the first line of the scene.

INTERESTING INTRODUCTIONS **[INT/WU]** – This is a great game for getting to know peoples' names. Form a circle. The first person alliterates their name (ex. Just Jackie or Super Sandy) and accompanies it with a gesture. The next player *only* repeats the previous person's alliteration and gesture and then comes up with their own. Continue until this ends with the first person doing the last person's name and gesture. *Variation*: Have each person in the group recall on *all* previous names and gestures in their correct order.

IT'S ALL RELATIVE **[FREIMG; IMPROV; CD]** - Suggest and idea for a monologue. Have an actor then perform at least a one-minute monologue on this idea. At the conclusion of the monologue, two or more people improvise a scene based on this monologue. Follow up this scene with another one related to the first two performances. At the conclusion of the scenes, end with a monologue and tie-up the entire idea/sequence.

JACK **[INT/WU; CONC]** - This fun warm up game will loosen up players. Form a circle around a single person called the "caller". The caller points to someone in the circle and assigns them a letter. That person must come up with a name, object or service, and a location all starting with that letter. For example: "J" **J**ack **j**uggled bottles in **J**apan. Anything is acceptable as long as it comes out instantly; otherwise the actor Must replace the caller in the center of the circle.

JUST YES AND **[CONC; FREIMG; IMPROV]** - Two or more actors decide on a relationship and a location. Each line must begin with "Yes, and…"

LAST LETTER CHALLENGE **[CONC; IMPROV]** - Two actors play a scene. An actor's line must begin with the final letter of the other actor's last word.

MOVE IT MOVE IT **[IMPROV; USPC]** – Two or more actors play out a scene from a group suggestion. All actors must perform a movement or gesture with every line they speak.

MUSICAL STORIES **[FREIMG; USPC; GTY]** - Play music. The actors must perform a scene in sync with the emotion of the music.

ONE WORD AT A TIME **[INT/WU; LIS; GTY]** - All actors sit in a circle. Select a well-known story such as a fairy tale or a famous film. Make sure everyone knows its plot. Each actor must then recite one word of the plot until the story is told.

PILE **[INT/WU; IMPROV; FREIMG; LIS]** - At the start of a session, everyone writes down three sentences, each on a separate sheet of paper, folds them in half, and puts them in a pile. The sentences do not have to be related to each other in any way. Each actor then pulls three random sentences from the pile and puts them into his pocket *without reading them*. Two or more actors play out a scene with conflict. At random intervals the leader should ask the actors in the scene to read one of the sentences. The object is to incorporate each sentence into the context of their scene and work it into their plot. Some actors preface the random sentence with something like: "My mother always says…" or, "The motto I live by is..." *Variation*: The actors can decide for themselves when they want to pull a sentence, but they still must integrate the sentence into the scene and justify what they say. (Note: Scene scenario suggestions for this game are listed on page 140 in the Improvisation section of this book.)

PUDDING GAME **[EMO]** – Hand an actor pudding mix instructions and secretly assign him an emotion. The actor must read the instructions with the emotion. The others in the group must try to guess the emotion. *Variation:* Have the actor read a short nursery rhyme.

QUESTIONS ONLY PLEASE **[CONC; IMPROV; LIS; CD]** - Two actors perform a scene in which every sentence must be in the form of a question. If someone utters a statement instead of a question, they are replaced by another actor who continues the same character in the scene. The questions should contain information that fuels the scene and builds a story. *Variation*: Each actor can only say four words each time they speak. No less and no more. The number of words per sentence can vary upon your preference.

THE REPLACEMENTS **[LIS; FREIMG; CONC]** - Start a scene with two to four actors. Halfway through the scene, the leader will say, "freeze." All of the characters will then be replaced by new actors. The new actors will take over the original characters and stay true to the story.

SAY SEVEN THINGS **[INT/WU; FREIMG; IMPROV; CONC]** - A group of actors stand in a circle. One person points at any random person and asks them to name seven specific things. (For example: "seven things you take in the tub" or "seven things you find in a glove compartment.") As that random person lists off each thing, the entire group counts aloud until the person reaches a total of seven things. That person then chooses the next random person and asks them to list seven things of their choosing. This continues on until everyone in the group has listed seven things.

SCULPTING **[GTY; LIS]** - This game uses three actors. One actor plays the model, the second is the clay (the potential sculpture), and the third plays the artist. The model poses behind the clay. The clay must not be able to see the model. The artist must form the clay to match the model's pose. The artist must do this without speaking, touching the clay, or imitating the model. When the artist is done, the model will inspect the sculpture.

SING THOSE WOES AWAY **[FREIMG]** - Come up with a ridiculous problem. Two actors play a bartender and a patron. The patron goes into the bar and sings about his problem to the bartender. The bartender in turn sings a new song of advice to the patron fixing his problem.

STEPPING IN **[INT/WU; FREIMG]** – Two to four actors begin a scene. An outside actor should step forward pausing the action. The actor who stepped forward repeats the last line said in the scene and replaces the actor that had said the line. A new scene should begin based on that line. *Variation*: When the replacement steps in, the same scene can continue.

STORYLINE SUGGESTIONS **[FREIMG; IMPROV; LIS]** - This game requires two to four actors playing out a scene. A minute or two into the scene, the group leader claps his hands and the actors freeze. The audience suggests how the story should continue. Continue the scene, incorporating these suggestions. This can be repeated throughout the scene. *Variation*: The audience supplies a new emotion instead of a new storyline.

SWITCH IT UP **[CONC]** - Two to four actors play a scene. When the group leader calls "switch," the actors all change roles. Start with two actors and add one more to each game to increase the challenge.

TALL TALES **[CD; FREIMG; USPC]** - One actor gets on stage and tells a story, playing the narrator, and acting out all of the roles in the story.

TAP TAG **[IMPROV; LIS; INT/WU]** - Two actors play a scene. At any point during the scene, an outside actor can tap the shoulder of one of the actors in the scene and replace him. The scene continues along with the tagging in until the scene is over. *Variation*: When an actor replaces someone, a new scene begins but the character from the old scene is still the same character in a new scene.

TRANSLATING TERMS **[INT/WU; FREIMG]** - All actors sit in a circle. One person says a word in gibberish to the person at their right. That person makes up a definition for this word and then creates his own gibberish word for the person at his right, and so on. *Variation*: Add a language origin to the word given. Also, consider stating the part of speech and using the word in a sentence.

ULTRA REMIX **[INT/WU; EMO]** - Split the group in half. Have one group play out a scene from a well-known story or fairy tale. The same scene will then be played by the other group but incorporating the opposite emotion (depressed and exuberant), tone (optimistic and pessimistic), traits (young and old), or style (Old English and modern English). The same scene can be replayed by the original group with new criteria. This can be repeated by each group several times.

UNIFORM FREEZE [INT/WU; USPC] - All actors meander about the room. Whenever one person stops, everyone immediately freezes. As soon as everyone freezes, everyone resumes their wandering. *Variation*: Actors can sing, hum, stomp, chatter, or make any noise they want. The louder the room is, the more challenging this exercise will be.

WEEE THREEE RULES [CONC; LIS] - The group makes up three rules. Two to three actors play a scene following those rules. (Examples of rules: no one can use the word "the," actors can't use their left arm, and after every question asked, the actors need to yell, "No way!")

WHAT'S YOUR SIGN? [INT/WU; FREIMG] - Hand out horoscopes to each actor. Have them create a scene based on the horoscope.

WORD CHAIN GAME [FREIMG; INT/WU] - All actors sit in a circle. One person says a word. The person to their right then says the next word to pop into their mind. This continues around and around the circle. (For example: cat, food, grocery, store, shopping, etc.)

ZIP, ZAP, ZOOP, AND BOING [INT/WU; CONC; LIS] - Players stand in a circle. The starting person will say "Zip" to the person next to them. He will say "Zip" if he continues in the same direction or "Zap" to reverse the direction. Pointing and saying, "Zoop" throws it to anyone in the circle. "Boing" bounces the flow of the game back to the person who spoke last. If anyone messes up, they are "out" and a new round begins.

ZIP, ZAP, ZOP **[INT/WU; CONC; LIS]** – Actors form a circle. One selected player starts by points to any player, and says, "Zip." That chosen player then says, "Zap" to someone else. That third player points to another actor and says, "Zop." This continues on and on until someone messes up. Any player who hesitates too long or says a word out of order is "out" and a new round begins until only one victor remains.

Great Games and Exercises for Scene Work: Some of the aforementioned exercises work really well for scene work. These "scene work-shopping" games are listed here again, but the definitions vary slightly so they can be effectively applied to working on scripted scenes.

ANNOYING PERSON **[CONC; LIS]** - Actors play a scripted scene. Another person steps in and attempts to distract and annoy the actors in the scene. This can include getting in their face, yelling, asking questions, being in the way, etc. The actors in the scene must do their best to concentrate, ignore the annoying person, and continue their scene.

BEFORE AND/OR AFTER **[FREIMG; CD]** - After a scripted scene is played out, the actors ask the rest of the group (their audience) if they'd rather see what happened before or after the scene they just saw.

Variation: You can do it all: before the scene, the scene again, and after the scene.

GIBBERISH REPEAT **[CD; LIS]** - Two actors play out a scripted scene (or a short portion of a longer scene) and then do it again speaking in gibberish.

JEKYLL AND HYDE SCENES **[CONC]** - Two actors play a scripted scene where one of the players acts with a normal demeanor while the other player behaves abnormally.

MOVE IT MOVE IT **[USPC]** - In this game all actors in a scripted scene must perform a movement or gesture with every word or line they speak. Try to make the movement as purposeful to the character and situation as possible. If an actor does not move while they are speaking, the scene starts over again.

SWITCH IT UP **[CONC]** - Two to four actors play a scripted scene. When the group leader calls "switch," all the actors must then change roles.

EMOTIONS AND CONFLICT

It's different now that I have children... There's a whole world of emotions that are given to you when your children are born that you just didn't know existed before. I just put myself in the character's place, and into their predicament or into their moment of grief or whatever it may be. And then I just try as hard as I can to find what my character is feeling in myself.

— Kate Winslet

It's about breathing. Breathing the rhythm of whatever emotion you are trying to emulate. I swear anybody can do it if they become familiar with a particular type of breath pattern that emulates a particular emotion. That's the foundation [in teaching anyone to act].

— Mel Gibson

When you are playing a character with such emotional range, you are not quite sure where you should be. It requires a certain amount of kindness in a director to gently get you there. If they push you there it won't be organic.

- George Clooney

Our emotions are what make us human. A lack of emotion turns us into monsters. Emotion is a basic ingredient in drama. Some emotions are wonderful. Others are devastating. Portraying these emotions honestly is the essence of acting.

Without conflict, there is no drama. Conflict requires emotions to be at their peak. The writer creates the conflict, and the actors must convey the conflict through their portrayal of the character and their emotions. Even when the script calls for an intellectual conversation with little overt conflict, an actor must convey an accurate emotional underpinning to be believable.

We need to understand how we express our own emotions to understand how our characters express *their* emotions. Different stimuli evoke different emotions, depending on the character and their background. The Art of Communication in Acting section of this book on page 25 covers this issue in more detail.

The intensity or the way you project your emotions, will vary depending on what medium you are acting in. Your gestures can be much more slighter when working in film or TV. In a close up shot, you can show the way you feel in the way you shift your eyes. If you were playing the same character on stage for an audience of five hundred people, you might have to rely on more movement than just the look in your eyes. On stage you have to project what you're feeling on a larger scale. Gestures will often have to be bigger and sometimes more obvious. So, consider your audience and be sure to project appropriately. If you need to change anything, the director will certainly guide you.

Of course, there is much more to portraying emotions than simply implying how you feel and lessening or intensifying the way you present them. Indicating an emotion might be a good place to start for some actors, but you should always have your emotions rooted in something deeper as you become more experienced with acting.

Many actors are curious about how they should handle crying, kissing, or dying in a scene. And some novice actors underestimate how difficult projecting laughter in a scene can be. Each of these actions should come *naturally* when you are in character and in the moment. Most of the time, a good director or acting coach will guide you on how to achieve authenticity in such circumstances. The script and the director can also tell you how much intensity to put into the given action. Take into consideration what circumstances are surrounding the particular action. For instance:

Crying
- Is your character sobbing?
- Or is your character weeping?
- Is your character trying to hold back tears?
- Do tears have to surface?

Kissing
- Is the kiss you need to portray a passionate kiss that has finally occurred after years of longing?

- Or is it a meaningless drunken kiss?

Dying
- Is your character's death going to happen peacefully with loved ones at their bedside?
- Or is the death of your character going to be tragic and abrupt?

Laughing
- Is your character mildly amused and laughing genuinely?
- Or is your character finding their situation outright hysterical?

There are subtle and not-so-subtle differences with all of these actions. Use the director's notes, the script, and your connection with the character and situation to bring any of these actions to life.

Always remember that your motion should be purposeful. If you can't find a way to make something work for your character, it will end up looking forced, fake, and false.

Here are some tips and techniques to further understand how to get to the root of emotions in acting:

- **PEB (Personal Emotional Bond)** - When you use a PEB, you can sympathize with your character because you have been in a similar circumstance. This creates an instant understanding and triggers within you a real emotion, even sometimes bringing to mind a physical memory. Understand that memories can sometimes stop working in triggering the emotion you desire to achieve. As time passes and we age, the past holds different meanings and produces different emotions. If this happens, use a different memory or use visualization as a tool.

- **Visualization** – A powerful technique that can make your scene emotionally alive and can often give a character more realistic dimensions. Visualizing a circumstance can be more powerful than using a personal experience. You can choose to daydream about a scene directly from the script, or something alluded to from the script, or something you completely made up just to build on your character more deeply. The key to visualizing something efficacious for your character is to experience it behind your own eyes. It is not as effective if you watch your character's scene play out from a bird's eye view. Engage all five of your senses and freely watch the events unfold in your imagination. Have a sense of where you want to go with the daydream to achieve the desired effect, but let it go where it may. Don't rush it.

- **Comparison** – Comparisons or "comps" can be used in the moment (or perhaps mid-scene). If you don't have a PEB to use and visualization isn't working for some reason, you can think of a "comp." Sometimes you can't relate to how a character feels because you don't have that personal experience. Or sometimes, the things you visualize just don't quite "get your there" emotionally when you're in a pinch. When this happens, you must think of another situation (personal or made-up) that is *comparable* to what your character needs to feel. Imagine your character opens a chest and finds a wide array of bloodied body parts – and your character is absolutely thrilled at this discovery. Chances are you, personally, aren't at all thrilled to find such a thing. So you have to imagine it is filled with all of your childhood toys and memories that you thought were long gone. You just need to be emotionally thrilled to the same degree as your character.

- **Actioning** – This technique can transform a non-specific piece into something richer and more meaningful. Sometimes it's hard to get into the character's head and understand how to say the words you're given. A technique often used by actors is called "actioning" the text. You will want to go through your script and assign a transitive verb to each sentence. When you do this, it will help you to zero in on what the character is really trying to say and do. Everything stems from love or fear. When I'm not sure of how to begin looking for the right transitive verb, I ask myself if the text in question stems from love or fear and I start to narrow it down from there. A fantastic book to help with this technique is called: *Actions: The Actors' Thesaurus* by Marina Caldarone and Maggie Lloyd-Williams.

- **Trigger** – Coming into a scene after using a "trigger" basically means that you are set in the proper emotional state of mind right from *before* the start of your scene. Quite often, if an actor isn't prepared before they go on, they tend not to be emotionally "warmed up" to the situation until they get halfway through their scene. You want to start off completely engaged in the character's circumstance and state of mind. As Sanford Meisner often said, "Don't come in empty!" You can use an assortment of "triggers." Think of something from your personal life or a certain emotionally stirring song or just visualize a situation to generate the right emotion. If you need to go off and be alone for a few moments to focus on your trigger, make sure you do so. As long as it gets you where you need to emotionally be, it doesn't matter what thoughts you are using as your trigger. All that matters is the genuine honesty of the emotion to get you started.

- **Alba Emoting** – This technique breaks down what physically happens to you when you experience specific emotions and teaches you how to apply it to acting. The nice thing about using Alba Emoting is that it takes away the mental anguish actors might need to put themselves through to give a powerful performance. Alba Emoting takes quite a bit of training, but once you acquire the training, the result is often quite impressive. Actors that have used Alba Emoting effectively have been known to give striking performances with engaging focus and undeniable power. The six basic emotions (happiness, sadness, fear, anger, eroticism, and tenderness) are taught through patterns of breathing, facial expressions, and posture and/or bodily tensions. The seventh pattern is a neutral state called a "step-out" which basically cleanses the actor's emotional palate. The "step-out" can be a necessary step, as some of the emotional patterns get very intense. Perhaps the most impressive idea behind this technique is that it is based on universal attributes that transcend culture, history, and psychology.

The technique itself can get quite technical, so it best to learn more about it through taking classes with a certified instructor. The overall method is taught in phases. In the first phase, an instructor will teach you how to robotically approach each of the six emotional states through breath, facial expression, and bodily tensions. The second phase is an induction phase where the student associates the subjective feeling. In the final phase, everything comes together and is incorporated into acting. To learn more about Alba Emoting, visit either breathxpress.wordpress.com/alba-emoting/ or albaemotingna.org.

- **Fake it Till You Feel It** – It may sound outrageous, but it does lend some credibility. I think it can be very useful to novice actors. It can also benefit experienced actors who are having a difficult time "getting there" emotionally. One of my acting instructors used to tell my class to "fake your emotion until it becomes real." It sounded preposterous, but I found that it worked for me. I started out indicating a difficult emotion for me to access, like sadness and crying, and a few moments later I wasn't indicating at all. Real tears were emerging from my eyes. My body began to shake, my face began to flush, and my spirit fell at the mercy of the sadness that enveloped me. It all started fake and blossomed into something very real. Then I learned that studies and experiments have shown that when you make a facial expression that represents a certain emotion, you can actually bring on those real feelings and emotional states. However, I wouldn't recommend starting a scene in front of an audience in "fake mode." Start faking it before you enter the scene. Get into the proper frame of mind before it starts. Then, if you can, enter the scene with the real emotion.

Even when you feel you finally have a lock on the emotions your character experiences, remember to always stay open to anything that comes to you in the moment. Anything new that comes into the scene should be welcomed with unsurprising, natural ease. Always let the character have the freedom to speak through you in any way he wants. There is no such thing as doing it "wrong," as long as the emotion is real and appropriate.

You always want to aim for full believability. If you are connecting with your character and your circumstance, your audience will be connecting with you.

Take all or some of the emotions listed in the following section and transfer them onto little slips of paper. Take all of the slips of paper and fold and place them in a container or bag. This is your collection of emotions you can use in a variety of different exercises. When playing with these exercises, try to really fall into the shoes of your character and feel as they would feel in the given circumstances. Try to avoid the trap of indicating an emotion and, instead, really feel the reason behind it. Here are some suggestions for exercising emotions using your new collection.

EMOTION EXERCISES:

Ridiculous, Please - In this exercise, all members of the group sit in a circle. One person pulls an emotion out of the bag and says either "ridiculous," "please," "incredible," "excuse me," or "excellent" with the selected emotion to the person on their right. The person to their right has three guesses to name the emotion. If he can't guess the emotion after three guesses, the entire group tries to guess. When the emotion is revealed, the person to the right selects an emotion from the bag and then says the same word to the person at their right with the new emotion.

Hush - This exercise forces us to discover and interpret emotion through facial expressions, mannerisms, posture, and physical presence. In this exercise, the group will each take turns pulling an emotion from the bag and expressing this emotion physically (with absolutely no vocals) to the group. The group calls out what they believe the emotion to be. Once the emotion is revealed, the next actor pulls a new emotion and performs his silence skit.

Generic Scenes – Pair up people in your group and ask them to find a relationship, location, and situation to incorporate in one of the generic scenes listed later in this section. The actors should also pull one emotion out of the bag and use the emotion as a basis for one of the characters. The rest of the group will watch the scene and afterwards will collectively attempt to guess the portrayed relationship, situation, and emotion.

How That Makes Me Feel – Each actor pulls one emotion and one noun (noun suggestions are listed on the following pages). Have each person create a short monologue or scene (they can choose a partner if necessary) that explains why the noun makes him or her feel the emotion they pulled. Make as much sense as you can when you relate the noun with the emotion. For example: "envy" and "bicycle" could be a quick skit about your character coveting his friend's new bike. The rest of the group will then try to guess both the noun and the emotion.

EMOTIONS:

Abandonment
Ambivalence
Amusement
Animosity
Anxiety
Appreciation
Apprehension
Arrogance
Awe
Bitterness
Boredom
Callousness
Calm
Cheerfulness
Cockiness
Compassion
Contentment
Cruelty
Deceptiveness
Delight
Depression
Devotion
Disgust
Distractedness
Distrustfulness
Eagerness
Egotism
Enthusiasm

Envy
Excitement
Fatigue
Fear
Frustration
Guilt
Happiness
Hate
Impatience
Joy
Kindness
Loathing
Loneliness
Love
Misery
Nervousness
Optimism
Panic
Peacefulness
Pigheadedness
Pity
Pleasure
Pride
Rage
Repulsion
Sadness
Serenity
Sexiness

Shadiness
Shame
Shyness
Skepticism
Slyness
Smugness
Sneakiness
Snobbery
Sorrow
Sternness
Stress

Strictness
Stubbornness
Strain
Suspicion
Tension
Terror
Vanity
Weariness
Woe
Wonderment
Worry

<u>**NOUNS:**</u>
Apartment
Apple
Bag
Bills
Brush
Cake
Chair
Clouds
Desk
Dog
Elevator
Floor
Gate
Gnats
Hair
Hammer
Illness
Joke
Koala
Ladybug

Lamp
Lighter
Mask
Morning
Neighbor
Office
Pantry
Pants
Quilt
Rain
Soap
Sun
Sleep
Table
Temper
Tent
Tractor
Umbrella
Voice
Wagon

GENERIC SCENES

Questions to ask yourself in a generic scene:
- Where are you (place)?
- What is your relationship? (Who are you? Who is your partner?)
- What do you want from your partner (motivation)?

A: You are late.

B: I know. But I really couldn't help it.

A: I guess I understand.

B: I thought that you might.

A: I have something for you.

B: You do?

A: Yes, this.

A: Do you have any idea what time it is?

B: Not a clue. What time is it?

A: It's almost three, where have you been?

B: Out. Just out walking and thinking.

A: Really? Thinking about what?

B: About what had happened.

A: Yeah, what about it?

B: I don't know.

A: Forget it.

A: Hey.

B: What?

A: What happened in here?

B: It looks all right to me.

A: Who did this?

B: Did what?

A: Look! How did that happen?

B: Oh. I see.

A: Oh my…

B: What?

A: Come here – come here!

B: Why, what happened?

A: Look at this. Can you believe it?

B: Wow.

A: "Wow" doesn't even begin to cover it.

B: I can't believe it.

A: I don't get it.

B: Just let it go.

A: This is just unreal.

B: I know. But you just need to move on.

A: How do you just move from this? How can I…?

B: It isn't going to be easy. But you have to try.

A: I don't know if I can. Nothing will ever be the same.

B: True. But you aren't alone in this.

Warm-Ups and Games That Focus on Emotions:

ALPHABET THROW..........................82
GREETINGS AND SALUTATIONS……...85
HITCHHIKER.................................86
INTERESTING INTRODUCTIONS.…....87
PUDDING GAME............................89
ULTRA REMIX..............................91

CHARACTER DEVELOPMENT

Character reveals itself by how you do what you do.

— Sanford Meisner

Posture and physicality offer a lot to forming your character – the way you speak, respond, walk, etc. It affects things you never thought it would affect.

— Charlize Theron

At the same time when you're acting you have to be open, open, open, totally free of yourself, while you're making believe to be someone else. And you have to have gotten to know him very well from inside out.

— Ian McKellen

I always and build a history for each character, really try and create a full person. So that, hopefully, when an audience meets the character and sees them on the screen they really feel the presence of a well rounded individual and they can feel a sense of history and depth.

— Kate Winslet

Don't be different just for 'difference's sake' - but if you see it differently, function that way. Follow your own muse. Always.

— Morgan Freeman

    The best way to approach any role is with thorough character development. The more you flesh out a detailed history for your character, the better sense of reality and depth you bring to your performance. Think about it – you know how to play you. You do it everyday. You know how to act and what to say to different people in your life. You behave one way with your parents and another with your spouse. You approach a potential employer differently than you would an old friend. Your relationship and history varies depending on the circumstance you are in. The same goes for your characters. Your character's history will never be as detailed as your own, but you need to explore it to be authentic.

The script, character description, and dialogue will tell you a lot about who your character is. If you are playing a person from history you'll likely have other sources outside of the script to research. If the script is based on a book, you can often read the book for more details and insight into your character. If you know the playwright, they can usually divulge unknown bits and details that will help you bring your character to life. There plenty of resources for getting more information on your character, but when the well runs dry and you still need to flesh out your character, you'll need to rely on your imagination and intuition.

When you read the script for the first time, get an initial idea of who your character is. But as you become more familiar with the script, you'll gain even more depth and detail into what makes your character tick. Pay close attention to the feeling you get from your character. How do you feel about what the character does and says? How does the character feel about the circumstances he finds himself in? What choices does the character make because of those circumstances? How does all of that make you feel? After all, this character is going to be part of you. How much of you is in this character? Find part of yourself in the character. Go with your gut, your instincts, your intuition, your research, your preparation, and be in the moment when the time comes to perform. And always be open to anything that comes to you as you are developing your character.

Incorporating specific body language, speech rhythms, clothes, and props can contribute a large part of character portrayal in different situations. The script or director dictates some of these things, and some of these things are character add-ons put in place through the creative liberties of the actor.

Picture a slouching character and one with a stiff posture. What does each different posture say about each person?

Think about a person who speaks distinctly and one who talks very slowly. What might those things say about someone?

Now picture a woman wearing a tight red dress with a long fur coat over top. What might that say about her character? Now imagine the same woman wearing a baggy old sweat suit with a hole in the knee. How did that change your idea of her character?

The way you manipulate a prop can enhance your scene and further define your character. For instance, how a person chops carrots can convey his state of mind. Imagine the difference between furiously attacking the vegetable with a knife and leisurely slicing each piece. It may be the same knife, but how it is used can further define your character and circumstance.

So many subtle (and sometimes not-so-subtle) things can go into forming a full, well-developed character. The most mundane detail can greatly contribute to the bigger picture. No small detail is too tiny to ignore.

Break down the script and filter out all of the details. Find the action of the scene and play it. Doing as your character does will help you find the character. Use the questions and lists further along in this section to build more details for your character. Also use the advice and exercises in the Emotions and Conflicts section (page 95) as well as tips from the General Notes for Auditions section (page 50) to aid in making more discoveries of your character.

Think about the different perspectives of your character. What do the playwright and script notes say about the character? How do the other characters perceive your character? How do you perceive your character? And most importantly, how does your character see themself? That internal perspective of your character is vital. Imagine that a script describes a female character as an abusive mother. An abusive mother may not see herself as violent and hurtful in any way. She might feel as though *she* is the tortured one just trying to make things work. You have to play the character as the character sees themself, taking in all the other perspectives only to feed your knowledge as an actor.

Should your character have a specific condition, you'll not only have to research that condition, but it might be useful to personally expose yourself to someone who deals with such a condition. Any illness or addiction can have effects that you never imagined. Jobs, diet, and simple choices in day-to-day life are influential on a scale you might have never imagined. The fears and insecurities people live with may not be fathomed until you see it first-hand. The way you speak, dress, spend money, drive, sleep are all factors to consider when your character has a certain illness or addiction. Do you best to understand, as thoroughly as possible, how someone functions under such extraordinary circumstances and how it affects him emotionally and physically.

If you are playing a character with an accent, and you don't have a coach to help you with it, you'll need to find ways to perfect it on your own. There is a wide array of books and CDs available for purchase that break down how different accents sound and how to speak them with accuracy. Additionally, there are quite a few websites that offer advice and snippets of audio that demonstrate how to speak a specific accent. A good website to check out is accent.gmu.edu. Sometimes an actor may ask a native speaker to record all of the actor's lines. (Thanks to modern technology and the Internet, this is a very feasible task compared to the years before the Internet.) This particular approach really assists the actor to hear how each word is pronounced. Rewrite the lines phonetically. Also be sure to keep in mind the culture behind the accent. Accents aren't always about pronouncing each word with certain flair. Think about the overall style of the language behind the accent.

A Few Final Notes on Character Development

There will be occasions where you'll probably play an "extra" in a production. Don't feel the need to dig too deeply into who your character is. You can certainly exercise some ideas in your head, but don't let your character development get in the way of the production running smoothly. Some actors take character development too seriously when performing in background work and it can become annoying or distracting to the other people working on the production.

In theatre, and occasionally with film and TV you might be part of an ensemble where you will play multiple characters. For example, the play *The Laramie Project* typically casts eight actors to play over sixty characters. Try your best to flesh out all of your characters as much as you can. But when playing an assortment characters, you should find unique ways to easily and quickly induce the soul of each character. Actors find all sorts of ways to get in touch with their character. It could be through posture, a catch phrase, a word, an accent, a song, a picture, a breathing pattern, a certain way of walking, a voice, a mental image, or a personal object. Find something unique to summon a connection to each character.

Questions to Ask Yourself About Your Character:

1. What role am I playing? (The supporting best friend, the nosy neighbor, the antagonist's apprentice, the damsel in distress, etc.)
2. What are highlights of my character's past?
3. What are lowlights of my character's past?
4. What does my character most want out of life? Who does he have to get it from?
5. What would my character want more than anything?
6. What would my character never want to have happen to him?
7. What does my character enjoy?
8. What turns my character off?
9. How does my character speak?
10. How predictable is my character? Are there specific patterns of behavior?
11. How is my character physically represented? (Posture, movement)
12. What is my character's attitude to others? To the world?
13. What does my character do to get what he wants? (Manipulate, kill-them-with-kindness, submit and beg, etc.)
14. How does my character manipulate items physically? (Clumsy, handy, deliberate, etc.)
15. What determines how my character feels about other people he knows? Other people he doesn't know?

Questions About the Script:

1. Where is the story taking place?
2. What is the basic plot of the story?

3. What is the genre? What "feel" does the piece seem to have?
4. What is the theme of the piece?
5. How are the interactions between characters portrayed?
6. What are the circumstances my character finds himself in?
7. What does my character want?
8. How does my character feel about the situation(s)?
9. What does my character have to endure?
10. Who does my character have to rely on? Betray? Interact with?
11. What kind of relationships does my character have? How does he feel about them? How does my character "use" others?
12. What obstacles does my character have to overcome? What will he do to get what he wants?

An Interview as Your Character:

You can do this on your own or interview people in your group, class, or cast. Answer these questions in character. Do not break character. Answer as honestly and as swiftly as possible. Don't look at the questions ahead of time. Try to be consistent.

1. What is your name?
2. How old are you? When is your birthday?
3. Where do you live?
4. What do you do there?
5. What is your best attribute?
6. What would you like to do? Your dream job?
7. What kind of music do you like?
8. Where was your last vacation?
9. Where are your parents?
10. Where did you grow up?

11. How much money do you have on you?
12. Are you poor, middle class, or rich?
13. How much sleep did you get last night?
14. What is you favorite thing to eat?
15. What did you have for lunch today?
16. Do you exercise?
17. What are the biggest influences in your life?
18. Are you well liked? Do you have any positive relationships?
19. Are you well educated? Do you have any degrees?
20. What's your pet peeve?
21. What do you appreciate more than anything?
22. What would you get rid of if you could make anything in your life disappear?
23. Where are you going from here?
24. What's your favorite movie?
25. Would you ever kill someone?
26. Are you in debt?
27. Do you pay your bills on time?
28. Do you shower daily?
29. How often do you brush your teeth?
30. Do you (or did you) do well in school?
31. Are you an introvert or extrovert?
32. Who is the closest person to you? Emotionally?
33. Are you married and enjoying it? Do you ever want to be?
34. Do you have (or ever want) children?
35. What are your political views?
36. What is your religion?
37. Do you drive or own a car?
38. Do you own a gun?
39. Do you have any pets?
40. Do you like adventure?
41. Are you an optimist or a pessimist?
42. How many hours do you sleep at night, on average?
43. Do you have any siblings?

44. Do you eat healthy?
45. Did you have a happy childhood?
46. Do you drink?
47. Do you smoke?
48. Do you or did you ever use street drugs? Prescription medication?
49. Do you wear perfume or cologne?
50. Do you wear a watch? Any jewelry?
51. What do you do on weekends?
52. Do you or did you ever have any major medical problems?
53. Who is your best friend?
54. Who is your idol?
55. Do you consider yourself to be attractive for your age?
56. What is your biggest fear?
57. What is your favorite color? Why?
58. Who was the closest person to you that died?
59. What are your hobbies or interests?
60. What accomplishment are you most proud of?
61. What three words describe you best?
62. If you could be anyone or anything, who or what would you be?
63. What was your first job?
64. What is on your bucket list of things to do before you die?
65. Have you ever broken any bones?
66. Where are your ancestors from?
67. What is your taste in clothing?
68. How do you normally wear your hair? Do you dye it?
69. Do you remember your dreams when you wake up in the morning?
70. Have you ever been truly in love?

FLESHING OUT YOUR CHARACTER:

Name of Character: _____

Time Period: _____

Script Title: _____

Vocal Qualities
    Quality: _____
    Pitch: _____
    Pace: _____
    Force: _____
    Special Mannerisms: _____

Physical Qualities
    Height: _____ Weight: _____
    Age: _____ Birthdate: _____
    Build: _____
    Posture: _____
    Health: _____
    Mannerisms: _____
    Walk: _____
    Attire: _____

Facial Qualities
    Eyes: _____
    Cheeks: _____
    Mouth: _____
    Nose: _____
    Forehead: _____
    Chin: _____

Complexion: _____
Hair: _____

Beliefs, Attitudes, Status

Ethnic Characteristics: _____
_____

Family History: _____
_____

Education or Degrees: _____
_____

Social Rank: _____
_____

Economic Class: _____
_____

Morals and Values: _____
_____

Philosophies on Life: _____
_____

Disposition or Temperament: _____
_____

Emotions Expressed Most Frequently or Easily:
_____
_____

Unusual or Outstanding Personality Traits: _____
_____
_____

Audience Attitude Regarding Character: _____
_____
_____

Plot and Relationships

What spot is the turning point of the script?

What do you believe is the theme of the script?

What point of the script is the most dramatic or climactic moment in the script?

What does your character contribute to this climax?

What is your character's point of view on life (or overall) in this script?

List the major characters that your character has interaction with. Also state your character's attitude toward each one and list the other characters' attitudes toward your character:

_____
_____
_____
_____
_____
_____

CHARACTER DEVELOPMENT EXERCISE:

I Know You - In this exercise, the group sits in a circle. The group leader passes out magazine clippings of individuals. Each actor in the circle has to come up with a name and description of who this person is and how he knows him. As he shows the picture to the group, he should embellish the back-story. The object of this exercise is to let the actors' imagination run wild, with developing details about the character in the picture.

Warm-Ups and Games That Focus on Character Development:

COMMON OBJECT...........................83
GIBBERISH REPEAT........................85
GREETINGS AND SALUTATIONS......85
HIDDEN QUALITIES........................86
HITCHHIKER....................................86
IT'S ALL RELATIVE.........................87
QUESTIONS ONLY PLEASE..............89
WORD CHAIN GAME........................92

GET IN TOUCH WITH YOU

Discover things about yourself in the public arena of a rehearsal, if you can do that, then you're likely to stumble over some truth about the character which relates to the truth about yourself and you'll be on the right track.

— Ian McKellen

Find in yourself those human things which are universal.

— Sanford Meisner

    Get in the habit of observing yourself. Be honest with yourself. The more truthful you are with knowing yourself, the better you'll be able to play another character.

    You need to be able to portray realistic emotions in response to your character's circumstances. How do *you* think and react to certain situations? How is that the same or different from your character? Pay attention to your posture. After interacting with other people, review what you said and how you felt. After an average day, consider how you felt and reacted to each situation that occurred. Were you comfortable? Think of how you felt, how you sat, how you looked, and how you spoke. It's important to be yourself and then reflect on it later. Catch yourself and observe your reactions whenever you can.

Your character's mannerisms could be vastly different from yours. Perhaps when you listen to a friend talk, you sink back into your chair and pick at your fingernails. But your character may lean forward and fold his hands. To know your subconscious mannerisms, you need to be in touch with yourself. You need to know your character and know yourself so you can understand how much of "you" is in your character.

How can you take steps toward knowing yourself a little better?

- **Keep a journal.** It doesn't have to be anything elaborate, but it will be beneficial.
- **Spend some time alone.** Go for a walk by yourself or take up meditation.
- **Make a list** of your strengths and weaknesses.
- **Write a synopsis** of who you are. Are you outgoing or shy? Open to change or resistant to it? Optimist or pessimistic? Are you very self-involved or aloof? Would you rather work alone or as a team? What are your dreams? Dissect yourself and elaborate.
- **Call someone** and catch up. After the conversation, review what you talked about, what you said, and how you said it.
- **Read** old journal entries, papers, or stories you have written in the past. As you read, you'll remember who you were and how that person compares to who you are now.
- **Watch old video footage.** There may be moments when you don't realize the camera is on you. Observe yourself. Did you learn

something new about yourself? Have you changed since that time?

Warm-Ups and Games That Focus on Getting in Touch with Yourself:

ABC GAME................................82
MUSICAL STORIES......................88
ONE WORD AT A TIME...............88
SCULPTING...............................90
WORD CHAIN GAME..................92

LISTENING

Listening is everything.

— Matt Damon

There's no such thing as nothing.

— Sandy Meisner

Silence has a myriad of meanings. In the theater, silence is an absence of words but never an absence of meaning.

— Sandy Meisner

    Whether or not your character is a good listener or a bad listener, it's important to understand that listening is key to every scene. Every moment that someone else is speaking and you're not, your body language and non verbal reactions are saying volumes to the other characters and the audience. Listening is more than hearing. Your character may only hear and never listen, but you, as an actor, must listen to the other actors and react as your character would.

    You must hear, understand, and react to truly be listening. It is often easy to fall into the trap of thinking ahead to your next line when you should be listening. If you are honestly immersed in the scene and are doing as your character would, listening will naturally fall into place. Listening usually gives you the stimulus you need to react honestly. And that is a *wonderful* gift.

More information regarding listening can be found in The Art of Communication in Acting section of this book found on page 30.

LISTENING EXERCISE:

THE STATUE – This exercise illustrates the importance of listening. Pair up with another actor and assign one person be a listener and the other to be the speaker. The speaker tells a short story of any kind – as long as it's something he can talk about for approximately two minutes. The listener is not allowed to respond in any way to what the speaker is saying, verbally or physically. The listener MUST listen but cannot smile, nod, or show any indication of their inner thoughts and feelings. The listener's job is to be as much of a blank wall (or statue) as possible. When the speaker is finished, the pair should switch. After that round, discuss how it feels. How did it feel to be the speaker and the listener?

Warm-Ups and Games That Focus on Listening:

ABC GAME.............................82
ABC SCENARIOS......................82
BING BONG BANG....................83
COMMANDEER........................83
COMMON OBJECT....................83
CONFESS................................84
GIBBERISH REPEAT..................85
HIDDEN QUALITIES..................86
INSTA-STORY..........................86
ONE WORD AT A TIME.............88

PILE..88
QUESTIONS ONLY PLEASE………...89
THE REPLACEMENTS……………....89
SCULPTING……………………….…90
TAP TAG…………………………...…..91
TRANSLATING TERMS………..……91
WEEE THREEE RULES………..……92

For Scene Work:

GIBBERISH REPEAT……………...…….94

FREE YOUR IMAGINATION AND CREATIVITY

"The secret to creativity is knowing how to hide your sources."

– Albert Einstein

"Creativity is allowing yourself to make mistakes. Art is knowing which ones to keep."

– Scott Adams

      It's easy to get stuck in a rut. Life can be full of mundane activities and monotony. It's also human nature to resist change. Sometimes it is just hard to think outside of our own box. That's where research, creativity, and imagination come in to help you develop your character and acting skills. You gain insight as to why your character has the preferences they do by using your imagination and building a back-story for them. Free you mind and let the ideas flow! The more free-flowing you are with yourself and your ideas, the more freely a scene, situation, or character will come to you.

      Creativity is a very useful tool. In order to build a history for your character you may have to get very creative. Creativity will also come in handy with improvisation (more on that in the next section).

Creative thoughts came easier to us as children. As we grew up over the years we were taught to conform and think inside of the box. Certainly conformity has its benefits, but our thoughts need to be freed. Fortunately, with practice, creative thinking can come easier to you.

Tips to Creative Thinking:

- **Brainstorm.** Think of every possible solution or scenario to a particular issue and write all of your ideas all down. Write out the issue into a statement and elaborate on it. Write the situation into a question and come up with as many answers as you can. Try to come up with at least ten solutions.
- **Always have something to record your ideas on.** Especially on your bedside table. Some of the greatest ideas come from dreams or from those relaxed thoughts just before you fall sleep.
- **Open a book.** With closed eyes, point to a random word. Figure out a way that this word relates to your situation. This can help build back-story. Variation: Ask a friend to say three words and find relationships to your character or situation that way.
- **Exercise.** There is no doubt that physical activity boosts brain activity. Regular exercise will benefit your mind and body.
- **Come up with an analogy** to your problem or situation.
- **Ask yourself what other people you know would do** in your situation. Your mom? Your best friend? Your neighbor?

- **Think of the most outlandish idea** you can use to solve your issue.

BOOST YOUR DRAMATIC IMAGINATION:

Create the following things in your mind using your imagination. Close your eyes and really focus on recreating these sensations:

Smells:
- Skunk
- An orange
- Fresh baked brownies
- Cigarette smoke
- A garage
- Gasoline
- Roses
- Garlic
- An old book
- Popcorn
- Camp fire
- Farm
- New car
- Fresh cut grass
- Soap
- Bleach

Sounds:
- Traffic at rush hour
- Warm summer day
- Thunderstorm
- Fireworks
- Piano
- Revving Engine
- Lawnmower

- Cracking knuckles
- Cows
- Nails on a chalkboard

Tastes:
- Chocolate
- Apple
- Hot buffalo wings
- Lemon
- Banana
- Black licorice
- Scotch
- Salt and vinegar chips
- Sour hard candy

Touch:
- Bunny
- Warm coffee mug
- Sandpaper
- Snake
- Brail
- Baby's skin
- Velvet
- Beads

Sight:
- Mountaintops
- Desert
- Ocean view
- Roof tops
- Sunset
- A distant view of city lights at night
- Stonehenge

IMAGINATION AND CREATIVITY EXERCISE:

Whodunit and How - Take the following scenarios and try to solve the "crime". Try to think of creative ways that the crime could have been committed. Come up with as many possibilities as you can.

- You wake up in the morning and find bird droppings all over your kitchen floor. You don't have a bird and all the windows and doors of your home are closed.
- You see on the news that a painting is missing at the art museum, and you later find it in your shed.
- You come home to find your garage full of helium balloons and a dead body sitting on a lawn chair.
- A man stole seventeen magenta bath towels from a linens store and ran from security officers.
- A fire in a field burns randomly into a perfect circle pattern.
- The playground equipment down town was pulled out of the ground with the concrete foundations still anchored to its bases.
- A car is parked upside-down in a parking spot.
- A woman forgot her purse on a park bench. When she went back for it only seconds later, a plate of cookies was sitting in its place.
- You come home to your empty house and the freezer door is wide open. All of your shoes are in the freezer and all of the food is missing.
- After shopping at the mall you walk outside to locate your car, and find it's been parked in a different spot than where you had parked it earlier.

Warm-Ups and Games for Freeing your Imagination and Creativity:

GIBBERISH MASTER...................84
HEARING VOICES......................85
IT'S ALL RELATIVE...................87
PILE..88
SAY SEVEN THINGS...................89
SING THOSE WOES AWAY...........90
TRANSLATING TERMS...............91
ZIP, ZAP, ZOOP, AND BOING.......92

For Scene Work:

BEFORE AND/OR AFTER............93
GIBBERISH REPEAT..................94

IMPROVISATION

"Say yes, and you'll figure it out afterward" has helped me to be more adventurous. It has definitely helped me be less afraid.

— Tina Fey

While we don't always have to improvise our way through a scene, sometimes it is a necessary skill when the unexpected happens. Someone misses their cue, someone forgets his entrance, a prop is lost, etc. Sometimes a director may ask actors to improvise during a scene. Whether or not you feel you're any good at improvising, it's never a bad thing to have some improvisation experience under your belt. It can free your mind and help you to learn more about your character.

The more you practice, the more comfortable you'll become with it. You'll find that the fun you have with improvisation will boost your confidence in acting, as well as in your everyday life.

Enriching Benefits of Improvisation:
- Gain more confidence
- Develop "team player" skills
- Increase acting skills
- Enhance public speaking skills
- Improve brainstorming capabilities

- Refine decision making skills
- Increase listening and observation skills
- Boost creative thinking
- Gain confidence in social settings

The great thing about improvisation is that there aren't any lines to memorize. The not-so-great thing about improvisation is that there aren't any lines. There is no plan. There is no rehearsal with a script and blocking. There's only you, your partner, your creative thoughts, and hopefully lots of practice. Most of the time, believability in acting skills can take a back seat. Improvisation is a form of "fun" acting. Feelings can often be indicated instead of truthfully felt.

Improvisation is usually done in the format of a game (see the "Warm Ups and Games" section of this book.) There is typically a structure and a set of rules that the player has to comply with. Quite often an audience suggestion is taken for the scene to take shape or direction.

Some people have a knack for improvising. Many of us need to work at it, practice frequently, and expose ourselves to it regularly to be successful.

Here are some improvisation tips:

- **Always add something to the situation**. Don't ask questions and put pressure on your partner(s) to come up with all of the details within a situation. Think of the words, "Yes, and…" to help you move the story along. Questions are often the culprit of not contributing information. If you're asking things like, "What is that?" or "Where are we?" or "What's happening?" you may be relying too much on everyone else to create the circumstances of a scene. If you are asking questions, be sure they are contributing information to the plot. Try to include as many details as you can when you are speaking: "Last year, dad told us not to camp by this creepy cave and now here we are again."

- **Agree with the circumstances.** Feel free, however, to create conflict within those circumstances. Don't struggle with your partner(s) to establish things. If you started with a pantomime of your character watering his flowers and your partner says, "I see you're taking your dog out for a walk." you are now walking your dog.
- **Imagine the environment around you.** Really *see* where you are. This will help you to "find" things to use in the scene. Mime objects slowly and purposefully to make them appear more realistic. If you rush your movement it can look too vague and can ultimately confuse the audience. And when you "anchor" an item like a table, keep it in the same spot and never walk through it.
- **Don't pre-plan your responses.** You need to work off of your partner's improve. If you try too hard to set off in a direction from the beginning, and your partner isn't aware of the direction that the scene is taking, the scene will fall flat.
- **Change is good.** If your character (or at least one of the characters in the scene) changes from the beginning to the end, it will be more entertaining. A skill like this often takes practice. No one wants to watch only one particular emotion or situation for an entire scene. Typically, one person starts in a high status and the other person in a low status. Watching the gradual shift of a high status character transforming into a low status character (or vice versa) is nearly always entertaining.
- **Don't feel the need to go for funny.** This is probably one of the largest misconceptions of

improvisation. In the end, the audience wants to see a good story. If humor pops up as a by-product of that story, then great! If not, then at least the story was interesting.
- **Practice stretching your mind**. If you can get a group together to practice improvisation or sign up for a class, it will greatly help to expand your skills. And even if you choose to practice improv on your own, there are some creative mind games you can play to exercise your brain. One such game is to point at random objects and call them anything but what they are (i.e. pointing at a chair and calling it an "eggplant"). If you do this for about five minutes a day, you begin to open up your mind to more spontaneous and creative thoughts.

Suggestions for Scenes with Conflict:

A **customer** must deposit a check immediately. The check is not signed. The **Banker** will not accept the check. Bank policy states that a check must be signed by an authorized signee in order to be deposited. The bank closes in five minutes.

A **Customer** tries to return an item without a receipt. The **Store Clerk** won't take back the item without the receipt.

A **Cop** pulls over a **Driver** for speeding. The driver believes he has done nothing wrong.

One **Neighbor's** dog keeps leaving "dog bombs" in the other neighbor's yard and doesn't clean up after their pet. The neighbor knocks on their door to complain.

Bobby stole some toys from Michelle. Michelle's **Parent** accuses Bobby's parent of Bobby stealing.

A **Tenant** calls a **Landlord** about another tenant's loud music. The landlord explains they have to work it out between themselves.

Neighbors in an apartment building have problems with the other neighbor's noise. Both are convinced the noise is intentional and set on aggravating the other.

Landlord and **Tenant** argue over security deposit and damaged items.

A **Patient** goes to the **Doctor's** office begging for an antibiotic for a sore throat. The patient has been sick for nearly a week, has no health insurance, and can't afford the doctor's visit.

Husband and **Wife** argue over who will take care of their crying baby. Both have work early in the morning and the baby has been crying all night. One argues to let the baby cry, the other says the baby has cried long enough.

Sisters argue over who has the next family picnic at their house. Neither of them wants to host the event.

Neighbors argue over their property line. One of the neighbors wants to put up a fence.

Siblings disagree about putting their parent(s) in an assisted living home.

A **Boss** tells an **Employee** he is taking too many personal calls at work. The employee feels that his personal calls are normal and less frequent than his co-workers.

A **Teacher** cannot accept a **Student's** generous gift.

Two **Strangers** in a parking lot argue over a scratch on one of their cars.

Two **People** living in close proximity: "I slipped on your sidewalk."

Siblings argue over watching the game on Thanksgiving. One wants to spend time with the family, the other doesn't want to miss the football game.

A **Couple** argues over sloppiness.

A **Daughter or Son** argues with his **Mother or Father** about taking his medications regularly.

Friends argue over why they have not been in touch with one another.

Co-workers argue over who has to take on the next big project. The boss is away and neither employee wants to do the data entry. Only one person can do it for consistency.

A **Couple**: It's their anniversary and he wants to go next door and watch the game. He offers to take her along. She wants to go out and celebrate as they had planned to.

Sam is irresponsible and no longer has a car. Sam asks **Pat** to borrow Pat's car. Pat is reluctant and says no. Sam doesn't understand why.

Kelly returns **Morgan's** new car. There is a scratch on the driver's side of the car. Morgan had reluctantly let Kelly borrow it for the day.

Two **Girlfriends** out shopping each spot the same dress they want for their next formal function (at work, at school, etc.) Both love it and neither person wants to get another dress, nor do they want their friend to wear the same dress to the function.

A **Father** argues with his **Son** about ruining his tools.

Two **People** argue over being lost on the way to an important meeting.

A **Young Man** wants to enlist in the army, **Another Man** (these characters can be related) tries to talk him out of this decision.

Two **people** argue over a scam. **Quinn** insists it's not a scam, and **Alex** has been taken and has proof. Quinn dismisses this proof.

Three **Co-workers** argue over who has to take on the boring and tedious portion of a large job that their boss has assigned to them.

A **Daughter** argues with **Parents** over going to the big school dance with a boy one of the parents does not like.

Warm-Ups and Games That Focus on Improvisation:

BING BONG BANG......................83
COMMANDEER........................83
COMMON OBJECT....................83
CONFESS................................84

FOREIGN FILM……………..……84
GIBBERISH MASTER…..………..…84
HEARING VOICES………..………..…85
IN CONCLUSION…………....…......87
IT'S ALL RELATIVE………..…......87
JUST YES AND………..……………....88
LAST LETTER CHALLENGE…..…..88
PILE……………………………...…....88
QUESTIONS ONLY PLEASE……….89
SAY SEVEN THINGS……………….89
STORYLINE SUGGESTIONS……….90
TAP TAG………………………….…...91

USE SPACE

An ounce of behavior is worth a pound of words.

– Sanford Meisner

    With both theatre and film, you must pretend that a fourth wall is there. It's not the audience or camera in front of you, but whatever is the setting for your story.

    You may have to look out over the heads of the audience and see a spectacular sun set or imagine you're at sea and your tiny boat is sinking. Regardless if you have a set or a blue screen, these places need to be "seen" by you. You need to feel like you're a part of the setting.

    Know your space. Be sure you have the right volume. Be sure you are using the potential of the space to work for your character and situation. Fill up the stage and the screen with your presence and your voice. Using space to its potential can be hard, but when a director gives you direction or blocking, it can enrich the scene. Some blocking choices may feel strange to you at first, but you should always find a way to make it work for the scene and your character. Make your motion purposeful!

USING SPACE EXERCISE:

Where am I? - Pick two of the following scenarios and decide how to create this location in the playing area. What activities would you do? How would you react? The rest of the group tries to guess your location and/or situation.

- In a mechanic's garage, diagnosing a vehicle.
- In a rose garden, fully in bloom.
- At the park by a fountain.
- In a forest.
- On a space shuttle.
- At the beach.
- At an orchard picking apples.
- At the top of the mountain, just off the ski lift.
- On a boat, preparing for a scuba diving expedition.
- At a Halloween parade.
- Shopping at an indoor mall.
- Erecting the framework for a new house.
- Picking raspberries.
- Planting a garden and prepping by pulling weeds.
- Visiting the Lincoln Memorial.
- Arriving at a hotel room.
- Boarding an airplane, finding your seat, and prepping for the flight.
- Grooming dogs at a pet salon.
- Working behind a desk at an executive office.
- Visiting the grave of a loved one at the cemetery.
- In a fire station as the alarm goes off.
- A police officer pulling over a speeding vehicle and then approaching on the side of a desert road.
- Sitting under the stars.

Warm-Ups and Games That Focus on Using Space:

ASSASSIN AND BODYGUARD.......82
COPY CAT WALK........................84
MOVE IT MOVE IT......................88
MUSICAL STORIES.......................88
TALL TALES................................91
UNIFORM FREEZE.......................92

For Scene Work:

MOVE IT MOVE IT ....…...94

CONCENTRATION

Success in any endeavor requires single-minded attention to detail and total concentration.

– Willie Sutton

Concentration is the secret of strength.

– Ralph Waldo Emerson

      Concentration can be tricky. You need to be relaxed and prepared to fully absorb yourself in your role. The art of acting requires that you know your lines and your blocking, but each time you perform you want to be fresh and real as though it was never done before. This takes lots of focus and concentration. However, you can't look like you're concentrating on anything. You have to be and remain in character, reacting realistically to imaginary circumstances. You can't break the "fourth wall." The blocking, cues, and lines must become second nature to you so that you can focus creating believable emotion and making your character real.
      Herein lays another challenge of acting. This is where being honest with the content of the scene and who you are comes in handy. The scene purely needs to flow. Personal issues need to be placed on the back burner. You need to put "you" aside and put everything

into your character. Be sure you try the following things to enhance your focus while acting:

- **Make lists.** This would include personal "to do" lists, as well as a list that summarizes your character's scenes, blocking, props, etc. If you have these important things written down it will take some weight off of your shoulders.
- **Get plenty of rest.** Fatigue will be certain to distract you. Make sure you get adequate sleep.
- **Try warming up.** If you haven't tried any relaxation techniques lately, you might want to see if that helps you get your head back in the game.
- **Go over your script.** Reviewing your lines and blocking will help you to focus.
- **Take breaks.** Depending on the demand of your role, this can be difficult. But try to find some time to clear your mind.
- **Give yourself some incentive.** If you can truly discipline yourself, come up with something special to reward yourself with if you successfully concentrate on your role.

CONCENTRATION EXERCISE:

INTERUPTIONS – Have someone from outside of the scene or monologue show interest in what is going on in the scene. This person should constantly interrupt and ask questions to throw off the actor performing. This exercise should encourage the actor to concentrate harder. (Similar to the *Annoying Person* exercise on page 93.)

Warm-Ups and Games That Focus on Concentration:

ABC GAME..............................82
ABC SCENARIOS......................82
ALPHABET THROW..................82
BING BONG BANG....................83
COMMANDEER........................83
CONFESS.................................84
COPY CAT WALK......................84
JACK......................................87
JUST YES AND.........................88
LAST LETTER CHALLENGE.........88
PILE.......................................88
THE REPLACEMENTS................89
SAY SEVEN THINGS..................89
SWITCH IT UP.........................91
TRANSLATING TERMS...............91
WEEE THREEE RULES...............92
ZIP, ZAP, ZOOP, AND BOING.......92
ZIP, ZAP, ZOP.........................93

For Scene Work:

ANNOYING PERSON..................93
JEKYLL AND HYDE SCENES.......94
SWITCH IT UP.........................94

ADDITIONAL QUOTES, ADVICE, AND THOUGHTS

Honesty isn't enough for me. That becomes very boring. If you can convince people what you're doing is real and it's also bigger than life. That's exciting.

— Gene Hackman

I'm curious about other people. That's the essence of my acting. I'm interested in what it would be like to be you.

— Meryl Streep

There is this big world of depth, and intrigue, and interest, and mystery with potential with every character you have. And it's up to you and your emotional intelligence to bring out that character.

— Jodie Foster

I think what I needed was to escape, frankly. Perhaps escape from the unhappiness of my mother's death, whether I realized it or not. Escape from the bullying that I suffered at school. Escape from my shyness into a world that was, at least for the two hours on stage, fixed, rehearsed, prepared, nothing could go wrong.

— Ian McKellen

Don't "over indicate" too much to help move along the overall plot. Think about the process, not the results.

— Matt Damon

If you really do want to be an actor who can satisfy himself and his audience, you need to be vulnerable."

— Jack Lemmon

You act with your soul. That's why you all want to be actors, because your souls are not used up by life.

— Stella Adler

IN CONCLUSION...

Every experience will give you something to carry on your journey of life. The same is true for acting. Things you learn in a class, from your peers, at a show, or through trial and error will imprint something on your soul. You take these experiences and use them, usually without knowing it.

We are all unique individuals and acting is not an exact science. The techniques covered in this book should give you a good foundation to work from. Some of the techniques will work really well for you; others may not assist you as much. Sometimes the effectiveness of a technique will depend on the character you are trying to connect with. We're an assorted lot of people, and our methods will always vary due to the differences in who we are. Some of us have an innate talent for acting; others have to work a little harder at it. But one thing is certain for most actors: if you have the passion for acting, there really is no better feeling than living in the moments of that passion. There are so many of us who do acting for the love of it, not the money. There is something very magical about that.

Remember the most important ingredients for success in acting: regular practice, confidence, perseverance, being prepared, positivity, permitting yourself to let go, connecting with your character, being in the moment, doing as your character would do, and using failure to motivate you.

Be honest with yourself about your abilities and with practice, preparation, and experience you'll become more comfortable with performing. The more comfortable and confident you are, the more your performance will benefit. Break a leg!

SECTION IV: MONOLOGUES, SCENES, AND ONE ACT PLAYS

All of the following monologues, scenes, and one act plays are written by Tesia Nicoli.

MONOLOGUES

FEMALE

Jess from *Tomorrow*
FEMALE 22-32
DRAMATIC

Jess is finally confronting her father on the guilt she feels he put her through.

(**Dad:** Jess, Where did we go wrong?)
Jess: We? You're kidding, right? (*Studies the look on her father's face*) You really don't know do you? It started with Emily. I mean, I get pregnant after being responsible enough to use birth control. My senior year was spent in trips to the doctor and lamas classes at night. And I was okay with all that. I finish high school and I graduate nine months pregnant – *with honors*. Tell me that was an easy thing to pull off. The day after graduation I go into labor. So I figure that's my destiny. I am not meant to go to college. Fine, I accept. Sweet baby Emily fills my heart with all the love I could ever ask for. My life has meaning. And then when I finally think I have everything figured out God wanted to take her away from me. Why? What on earth did she do to deserve going through *that*? When I first found out that I was pregnant, I was happy. Mom was supportive. I

wanted it to happen. It was meant to be – under the circumstances. Until the day I told you. Then my opinion changed. And then the doctors thought I couldn't carry her full term. So I prayed for it to be true! I prayed to lose little Emily because of your extreme disapproval of my pregnancy. That's the kind of hold you had on me. And two years later, my prayers were being answered. I was losing little Emily. You knew you'd love that little baby when she was here! Why did you have to be so cruel? There she was, so helpless, so still. All she needed was a chance. You never came to visit her in the hospital. You didn't call. You barely said anything when you came back from Hong Kong. I decided on her last day that I would never let you have a hold on me like that again. My whole life your approval was so important to me. And why? For what? Where did it ever get me with you? Todd could do anything at all and you supported him with open arms.
(**Dad:** Todd was different.)
Jess: We are both your children; he isn't any different than me! We are children and we needed the same amount of love and support. That's all I ever wanted! (*Calms down*) Look, I didn't want to get into this.
(**Dad:** No, no – I need to hear these things. Losing Emily didn't really hit me until she was really gone. I never thought she'd die. Children aren't supposed to die.)
Jess: So what's this visit all about Dad? You never come here to visit on your own. Mom is always with you. And when you do come with her you never talk. And when you do talk – I can tell you don't want to be talking. So, coming here out of the blue – alone and wanting to talk…it's just very out of character for you.

Lainie from *Modern Romance*
FEMALE 22-36
DRAMATIC

"Lainie"- finally confessing that she isn't as innocent as she seems.

Lainie: A while back I had a bit too much to drink. I met up with this guy. It was a night I went out with Lydia, well she left early. I was having a good time. And this guy I used to have a huge crush on was there too. A few drinks always fog the mind. My judgment was off. (*Pause*) It was a huge mistake. He worked at this bar and he pulled me into this room where they keep supplies. I really thought he was just going to show me a few things. Well, in a way he did show me a few things. I couldn't believe what I was doing, but one thing just led to another. I was so mad at Rich. I had to let it out. And I didn't want to let loose on Rich. Who knows what he'd do. I just had to find a way to deal with it. It was my way of letting it all go. But then it happened again. Not with that guy. It was a different time. A different guy. He was real sweet. He reminded me of Rich. In some ways that made it hard and in some ways that made it easy. But I felt a little less guilty after him. Maybe it was because he reminded me of Rich. Or maybe...since it happened before - I just knew what to expect.

Kathy from *Promise Me*
FEMALE 38-55
DRAMATIC

Kathy, who is a bit eccentric, poses a hypothetical scenario to prove how deeply she loves with all of her heart.

Kathy: Hear me out here, hear me out…an accident, purely an accident. Something that you could not prevent. Something that was tragic and she's hanging on by a thread. You spend weeks with your stomach in a knot. You're thoughts are consumed with "what if" scenarios. "What if I had done this differently?" "What if she doesn't live through this?" Your appetite is gone. Your digestive system is at a loss. Your bills sit and don't get paid. Your job suffers. Your health deteriorates. You forget to brush your teeth for days at a time. Because none of those things matter now. You sit at her bedside and watch her wounds turn black and things get worse. Hope diminishes. She's too weak to be operated on. And after weeks of intensive care she finally shows signs of pulling through. You get your hopes up and somehow through the grace of whatever God there is, she gets better. And you, in turn, get better. She gains consciousness…and strength. But, she's not the same. She's alive…but she's lost her mind. Her body is healthy as a whip, but her mind is gone, she doesn't remember you. She's lost all logical thinking functions. She can't work anymore, she can't drive anymore, she can't gauge how much to eat, or how to wash herself. She's essentially an infant again. So the question is: are you thankful she's alive anyway or are you the type that wishes she had died now that you see what she has become? What kind of person are you? And what really is more humane? Forcing someone to live like that or letting them go? Hypothetically, how would you feel? It's something you don't want to face. But – how can you truly appreciate what you do have – until you know what it's like to not have it anymore? The world is much simpler from a distance. So peaceful. But when you get up close...when you can see all the detail, it all changes. I love my husband and my children so much, that no matter what little piece of them is alive, I'd be devoted to them until I cease to exist myself. That is the kind of love I have with my family. And I feel so much love sometimes that I feel sick. And that is me. That is me.

Greta from *Smashing the Pumpkins*
FEMALE 25-35
DRAMATIC

Greta recounts her brutal revenge on a man who wronged her.

Greta: (*Slightly nods*) Don't get me wrong, it's not one of my prouder moments. I didn't plan ahead for it. It was opportunity knocking. It was knocking...it was knocking real loud. I couldn't ignore it. (*Pause*). I was walking back from buyin' a pack of cigarettes down at the Turkey Hill. I had quit smokin' about a year ago, but I started up again. I had to. I was walking down the dark street...it was late and I was exhausted. I hadn't been able to sleep for weeks at this point, you know? Every time I'd walk by George's house I couldn't help but be obsessed with him. Completely obsessed. I wanted to know where he was, what he was doing, what he was hiding, if he thought about what he did, if he regretted it, if he punished himself. If he could even get through a day, an hour, even a moment, without thinking about what he had done. Obsessed. While I was swimming in all of these thoughts I heard a door slide shut and a slight shuffle of footsteps. I was right walkin' by George's house. I looked over and George was standing next to his side door holdin' a garbage bag at his side and stopped dead in his tracks to look at who was walking down the street. His instincts told him it was me. He knew it. I stopped and starred at him for what felt like an eternity. And then this amazing calmness came over me. It was surreal. I never thought I'd feel that calm again. I'm not sure if I ever felt that calm before. He moved his hand back toward the knob on his side door and started to turn it. I said, "George, it's okay." And he stopped again. I saw him tilt his head like he was going to listen to me. I slowly walked over to him. "George...we can't live in the same neighborhood and ignore this issue. We have to find a way to...get along." He didn't believe me, but he didn't know what to do either. I caught him off guard. Now...I'm sure he was drunk. And I was so calm. I was right next to him and he set down the garbage bag. I think he started to say somethin' to me but I didn't wait to hear what it was. I pulled him off of his back porch. He fell faced down and didn't move. He didn't say a word. I grabbed him by the back of the head with my right hand...I grabbed him by a fist full of his long, greasy hair and I grabbed his arm and drove his head into the side of the neighbors house. It was a concrete wall. He tried to tell me that he didn't do anything, he pleaded with me, but that just fueled me more. I did that a few times, slammed his head into that wall...and watchin' his hair get redder under the light comin' in from the street...oddly it was one of the most invigorating sights to me. But after a few slams to the wall, I couldn't throw him into the wall as fast or as hard as I liked...so I looked around and found a large cornerstone on a pathway to the backyard of the neighbor's house. He didn't stir anymore. But I thought a few blows to the head from that cornerstone would finish him. Each thud sounded like freedom to me. You wouldn't believe the sound that it makes when you smash a stone against someone's head. It was a crowning moment for me. Justice. Justice! I finally felt better. But it didn't last. I was on auto pilot and soon after I was crashin'. It didn't change anything. It was only temporary relief. But... ultimately - I don't regret it. No (*laughs*), no, no, no, never! It was worth it.

Emilianna from *Everywhere and Nowhere*
FEMALE about 25-35
DRAMATIC

Emilianna talks to her long lost friend about what she went through with her ex-husband.

Emilianna: I didn't want to stay with Nathan, but he was the father of my little girl. I didn't want to move back to Quebec either. And I figured he only ever *threatened* to hit me, but he never actually did. In some sick way that was good enough for me. I remember him telling me, "You should be glad I don't hit you." That's a hell of a thing to be thankful for. He wouldn't let me teach Penny any English. If he heard me talk in English he would yell at me in French and tell me to only speak in French around her. I never wanted to move out of America, but I did it for him. I sacrificed everything for him. His violent tone finally turned physical one night. And it wasn't as if he just smacked me and felt bad. It didn't build over time. He thoroughly beat me and choked me the very first time. We had been married nearly six years on that night. He finally lost his mind and pushed my face against the cold tile floor in the bathroom. And he didn't care that Penny was not only in the house, but listening and watching. I don't want to get into detail…but let's just say that as I lay helplessly on the bathroom floor while he was choking me, I wasn't thinking, "Oh maybe tomorrow it will get better." I knew what I had to do. When he went out that night, I packed everything I needed for Penny and me. I called my parents and told them what happened…and what I was going to do. Then I called the neighbors, who heard everything by the way, and threw my suitcase from my balcony onto theirs. They hid it for me. The next morning when he went to work, Penny and I got on a flight to America. I was trembling with fear the whole time. I thought maybe he would find out somehow...and find me. When my family met us at the airport we collapsed into each other and just wept with relief for our safety. When I went to the doctor's office the next day, even the nurses cried when they documented my wounds. They told me that the cuts, bruises, and black and blue marks were nothing like anything they had seen before. They took pictures and wrote everything down for the trial. The divorce is final here in America. Nathan just needs to divorce me in Canada, and then the legal strings will be cut. He gets supervised weekend visitations with Penny. And... (*Beat*) that is what's new with me.

Stella from *Smashing the Pumpkins*
FEMALE about 30
DRAMATIC

Stella talks about the demon inside of everyone and why she got divorced.

Stella: Everyone has their demons. My ex-husband had a whole suitcase full of demons. He never showed them to anyone. Not even me. He kept them as a surprise for after the wedding. That's when I found out how insecure he really was. He asked me why I wore so much make-up. Why some of my shirts were so low cut (they weren't), why I moaned in my sleep, why I got home five minutes later from work on some nights, why I wore lipstick to the grocery store… it was exhausting Kate.
(**Kate:** I'm sure. I can only imagine.)
Stella: He didn't trust me at all. All the things he was originally attracted to me about were very things he wanted to change in me. I was miserable…you remember that time, don't you? I hardly talked at all on the phone when you called me…I'm so sorry. I basically locked myself up and felt I committed to the relationship…and I thought I needed to work it out. I thought he would grow up or change. I don't know what I thought. I'm just glad I got out and reclaimed my life. (*Beat*) Everyone's got their demons Kate. They're there whether we like it or not. Some people never show them. Some people let them out all the time. Some people only let them out on special occasions. It's the way of the human beast. I think it's inside all of us.

Gramma J from *Get Gone*
FEMALE 60-80
COMEDIC

Gramma J an older woman living at home with her grown son and his family explains why she's pretending to go crazy.

Gramma J: Yea, right…I don't know what's going on. (*Turns to speak directly to Ally*) I'm no threat. Half true. I DO know what's going on, but I am still no threat. My body is tired and old, but my mind is as sharp as it was 50 years ago. About ten years ago everyone in this house started acting like I was losing my mind. I got tired of it – and I started to play along. So, I have my reasons for pretending to be a mental loss. It's actually become kinda fun. Gives me somethin' to laugh about in bed at night.
(Ally: How terribly interesting. And very bizarre.)
Gramma J: I was just like you once. A stranger to this world. Then I met Itchy.
(Ally: Itchy?)
Gramma J: My husband, God bless his soul, his closest friends called him Itchy because he had an issue with scratching his - -
(Ally: I think I get the idea.)
Gramma J: One time he scratched with his gun and of course the thing went off, the bullet just barely missed his…family jewels. Left a big hole in his pants. (*Laughing*) Boy, we never let him forget that one. (*She sees Ally is not laughing*) Anyway…Itchy showed me the inside world. He and his friends were supposed to mug me, but he didn't have the heart to go through with it. A heart of gold, that one had. Long story short, eventually we casually dated. I tried not to fall in love. It was a forbidden love, like Padme and Anakin…Bella

and Edward...Mork and Mindy. *(Ally gives a puzzled look)* But it was meant to be none-the-less. Would you like to see some home videos?

Greta from *Smashing the Pumpkins*
FEMALE 25-35
DRAMATIC

After several therapy sessions and nearly a year after her daughter's death, Greta finally talks about one her last memories of her little girl.

Greta: (*Looks at Doc for a long time, takes a deep breath, and looks down at the floor recollecting a memory of Kelsie*) I remember her very last Halloween. She was five. In kindergarten. We carved pumpkins together. She made a huge mess, but that was really part of the fun. She loved eating the pumpkin seeds too. She loved those. She drew a funny face on the pumpkin and I helped her to carve it out. And I made one too. She was so proud. Kelsie asked me to take pictures (*Greta pauses to see the pictures in her mind*) and they were so cute. Her chubby little cheeks. That smile...with her tiny baby teeth, she never lost any teeth. Then she insisted that we put them outside and light them with candles. We lived on a main street...and we didn't have a porch...I warned her that it wasn't a good idea. But she was so proud. She wanted everyone to see the pumpkins we made. She wanted to decorate for Halloween. I knew she wanted to make the world a happier place by decorating it with what she made from her sweet, little heart. I put out the pumpkins. I didn't want to do it. (*Pause*) They lasted longer than I expected. And about two weeks later, when I saw the pumpkin guts smeared all over our front walk...I felt worse for Kelsie than I ever expected I would. She tried to fix the pumpkins, picking up the bigger pieces of the shell; of course it didn't work. She asked me what happened. And when I explained that that's just what some kids do...she just didn't understand. She cried and took it personally. We went upstairs and I told her we'd carve another one the next day. She stopped crying. She walked over to the front window and looked out at the street. Then she turned around and looked at me and said, "That's okay mama, we'll carve them again next Halloween and we'll put them in the window – so they can be safe." (*In a whisper*) So they can be safe.

Ally from *Get Gone*
FEMALE 22-35
SERIO-COMIC

Ally, a captive in Vince's home (a mafia gangster type), tells him a little about her upbringing. She is accompanied by Vince and a man that's badly beaten and gagged as well as tied to a chair.

Ally: (*Ally stands out of excitement and looks to Vince for approval*) Well, for instance, from what I can tell about your home, you should put a crystal in front of your door, because all of the chi is going right up your steps. The crystal would dispense the chi throughout your home more evenly...which is good. And you probably shouldn't keep a beaten, tied and gagged man in this section of your home. (*Indicating where Stegman sits*) That is your 'creativity and children' section of your home. Maybe put a duck over there. (*Stegman turns and looks at Ally with a bit of shock*) Ducks represent happiness. (*Ally gets and even better idea*) Or an elephant, they mean wisdom, strength, and power. (*Stegman silently weeps and looks down again. Ally sees Vince is starting to get into what she is saying*). Anyway, my Aunt Rosita lived by Feng Shui. She has things situated all over her home to enhance good fortune. She had a Bagua mirror over her front door to repel negative energy. You should get one of those. And she really believed that you must always keep the toilet seat down so that all the chi wouldn't go down the toilet.
(Vince: It can go down the toilet? (*Smirks*) No kidding.)
Ally: Yeah. (*Really getting into what she is saying*). And once in a while my Uncle Luis would make an occasional error and leave the toilet seat up, and a day or

so later Aunt Rosita would get sick. See, their bathroom was in the 'health and family' section of their home. Uncle Luis would always get an earful when he'd leave the toilet seat up. Aunt Rosita eventually made a really nice reminder sign to hang over toilet so that it wouldn't happen anymore.

Kate from *Smashing the Pumpkins*
FEMALE 25-35
DRAMATIC

Kate finally confronts Joe about his unreasonable behavior and the death of their friendship due to romantic feelings Joe has for her that she does not return for him.

Kate: Yes. But it was never you. I love you as a person. Not romantically. It was never romantic. It was brotherly. Remember when we went to that gorgeous park to see the fireworks on Independence Day? We sat together in that field waiting for the fireworks to begin and we talked about our separate lives. Our loves and loves lost. You told me some really intimate things about you and Sheryl. I thought we were onto something bigger than friendship. Maybe a fateful kinship. We understood each other, we could joke about things without all of those ridiculous complicated feelings getting in the way and spoiling it all. I thought we could conquer that whole "girls and guys can't be friends" thing. I thought that was going to be easy for us.
(**Joe:** Well it obviously didn't work.)
Kate: *You* didn't let it work. You decided to let in this rejection element. You had to fester up feelings that were never there! Why? Why couldn't you have just been there for me when I needed you most?
(**Joe:** Why? Why didn't you ever just give me a chance? We have what it takes.)
Kate: I wasn't feeling it Joe! I still don't feel it! All this pressure makes the potential to feel anything for you...it just...dwindles into nothing!
(**Joe:** So you're saying there was potential?)
Kate: Never mind Joe. Never mind. You proved the age-old theory. I thought we were stronger and smarter

than that. I thought we were above that. So I'm just going to take your advice. I'm just going to "screw off" as you so politely suggested.

MALE

Peter from *Smashing the Pumpkins*
MALE 68
DRAMATIC

Peter talks about dealing with his wife who is suffering from Alzheimer's as well as unresolved infidelity from many years ago.

Peter: Last week Mim called for me. She said she couldn't move her legs. She doesn't have a problem with her legs. She has a problem with her head. Her head is telling her that her legs don't work, but they do. I tried to help her out of bed. I was in and out of the bedroom all morning. I was trying to lure her with breakfast or a warm bath. Nothing was working. She kept complaining that she couldn't feel her legs. But she'd jump when I pinched her thighs. The whole morning was a struggle. I just…barely have the strength to do this anymore. Then she called me by *his* name. She didn't even know it was me. She thought I was Kevin. Remember that Kevin Milcot she claims she didn't have an affair with?
(**Alan:** I knew nothing about an affair. Really? Mim?)
Peter: Maybe not. I guess I kept that to myself. I didn't want to believe it. I thought I told you –
(**Alan:** The name sounds familiar -)
Peter: It doesn't matter. She called me Kevin all morning. I finally screamed at her. I lost it. Thankfully Kate was at work. "I'm not Kevin! I'm your husband, Peter! Your husband of 47 years! Now move your legs and get out of bed!" I yelled at her and she looked at me like it all dawned on her. I had her back for that split second. She looked at me with familiarity in her eyes. I

thought for sure she was going to snap back into it. I thought everything was going to come back to her. But then she screamed back at me, "Leave me alone you leach! You just leave me alone and don't come back in here!" It got her out of bed. She jumped to her feet and pushed me out the door. Slammed it behind me. I never felt so angry and so disgusted and ashamed with myself at the same time. At least I got her legs to work.

Gary from *Circumlocution*
MALE 35-45
DRAMATIC

"Gary" explains to an assisted living director how his life came full circle.

Gary: I didn't care about being a father. Not in the beginning. Drugs. I cared about finding drugs, buying drugs, and doing drugs. It didn't matter what kind I found, I'd do anything that I could get my hands on. That was what I lived for. There was this guy named Willie Tate, he stiffed me out of a lot of money, and I was tired of chasing after this guy. One night, I was so obliterated and so wound up; I went over to Willie's house. He answered the door and I just pounded away at his face. I hit the man until he was down and out for the count. Then I cut off the skin on his fingertips and toes with a serrated blade so that no one could identify him by his fingerprints. Then I realized that they could figure out who he was from his teeth…so I found a pair of pliers. (*Pause*) He woke up for that part. Funny, he didn't wake up for the skin, just the teeth. Then he got real quiet and limp. I threw him in an area rug, taped him up, and left him for dead in a dumpster down the street from his warehouse. The (*Laughs*) the bastard lived through that! Can you believe it? He lived through that! Man, if someone ever does that to me, I better die. Hey, don't feel too sorry for Willie though, he wasn't a model citizen by any means. He protested my release from prison. I couldn't blame him. Who could? But I've changed. I really changed my life around. Had a daughter. I finally got my baby girl. And I finally got to be a father to my boys. And then I get this disease. I guess this is karma. I thought prison was my punishment, but no…no…this is what's coming around for me. I change my ways, get all straight, and now I can't even brush my teeth by myself anymore. I can't take care of anyone. Not even myself. My kids are too young to support me. So, if you can't help me, I have nowhere else to go. Nowhere.

Ben from *Smashing the Pumpkins*
MALE 23-35
DRAMATIC

Ben notices that his friend Joe is showing a scary pattern of behavior toward a girl Joe desperately wants to date. Ben discloses to Joe an uncomfortable memory from his teen years.

Ben: You know, when I was seventeen, a long time ago, my mom had a stalker.
(**Joe:** Ben, where are you going with this?)
Ben: Hear me out, hear me out. She was terrified. We closed all of the curtains, no matter what time of day. We turned the lights out at night. We didn't answer the phone. We came and went out of the back door. We double-checked the locks on all of the windows and doors, even though we live in a second floor apartment. One day she smelled gasoline and she called the cops - -
(**Joe:** I didn't know any of this Ben.)
Ben: We waited outside until the cops came over. They checked the apartment and it was only a pilot light that went out in the stove, a slow gas leak. They fixed the pilot light and let us back into the apartment. She told me to go to my room. She told the cops everything. She didn't know I could hear the details, but I did. She was paranoid that this guy was going to burn down her home. And she went into all of the sordid reasons why she felt like he was capable of doing such a thing. She listed all of these things. Like when they dated he chalked her tires to know when she'd leave, he'd call her to check on her, he'd spy on her, follow her, call my grandparents, yell at any men who appeared to be too kind to her. Then the relationship got worse, he hit her. She called it off. He wouldn't let it go. He mailed her threatening

letters, pranked her...I remember some of this stuff, but I didn't grasp the severity - -

(**Joe:** I'm not doing this kind of stuff Ben - -)

Ben: He would drive by the apartment yelling things like "slut" as he rode by. And she told all of these things to the cops. She even showed them the letters. There was nothing they could do for her. So I stepped up and protected her. She wanted to protect me from worrying about her, but that was the day when I grew up. For the first time I didn't see my mother. I saw the scared side of an incredibly strong woman. You're not that guy Joe, but you could become that guy. You have this side to you that just snaps and all reason goes away. Don't do that Joe. Just don't ever be that guy.

Ron from *Burning Money*
MALE 40-60
DRAMATIC

Ron a CEO of a large coal mining company, justifies to a potential investor why he conducts business the way he does.

Ron: Look, Bill, I know we're not the greenest company out there. We mine coal. We use explosives to blow off mountaintops. But at the end of the day, it's a business just like every other business. Production has to be our number one concern. Without production, we have no business, without business we have no money, without money we have no economy, and the spiral just goes down from there. All of these green people complain about their water getting dirty and their air getting dusty, but you know they'd be the first ones to complain when their electricity doesn't work! You know it! And yes, people get hurt on the job, but that happens. And it happens in every type of workplace.
(Bill: There have been quite a few work related deaths with your company over the past few years.)
Ron: I'm not saying safety isn't a concern either. We don't want our employees hurt or putting their lives in danger, but they're paid well for what they do. Did you know the average wage of a coal miner is fifty thousand a year? Look, at the end of the day, we're a business. You're never going to please all of the people, so you just have to do what you can to produce the goods at the end of the day. Coal is the way of the future. Natural gas and oil are in limited supply. There are at least two hundred years of coal left. You can do what you want with your money, but I couldn't advise a better way to invest it than right here. And I'll never tell a soul.

Vince from *Get Gone*
MALE 35-50
DRAMATIC

Vince, a mafia gangster type, talks about justice and taking the law into his own hands.

Vince: Don't be afraid to voice your opinion. Stegman knows he was a very bad boy. He needs to start hearing it more. You see, Ms. Parker. Stegman had a Mommy who didn't care and a Daddy who cared too much...if you get the picture. He thinks people should suffer at his hands. They should be *his* puppets at *his* disposal. And he truly believes they deserve it. He is the center of his own universe. He is invincible. He is the one who decides if it is safe for you to walk down the street at night. He is the one who decides if you live or die. You see, Ms. Parker I often have good reason for doing what I do. I am doing the world a service – (*Seems pleased with himself*) in addition to my job. The system would shelter him, feed him and pamper his sorry ass for years in a prison. And if he was convicted, would it be for *all* of his crimes? Would they send him back out on the street due to that "beyond a reasonable doubt" crap? Even if he would change, does he deserve that chance? I am an old-fashioned fella – an eye for an eye. Well, Stegman has taken more eyes than he has. I know his crimes were real. Now I am the law. Do you still feel sorry for him?
(Ally: Well, I am a little sick about it. Of course, I could be sick for any number of reasons today. But why are you keeping him in your living room?)
Vince: He serves many purposes here. To embarrass him. To let him see how happy and functional (*Vince looks over at Gramma J who is bent over attempting to pick up an Uno card that fell onto the floor and she is*

also scratching her hind quarters rather deeply)…or…er…occasionally dysfunctional - a family could be. To show him a world that could have been his. And he's a good example to the kids, ya know, the consequences you pay if you screw up your life in a big way.

Roger from *Roger's Big Bad Day*
MALE 25-60
COMEDIC

Roger, who is generally quite laid back and willing to put up with anything, is fed up with being taken advantage of.

Roger: That's it! I can't find my Phillips head for the third time this week! (*Jumps down Nancy's throat before she even gets a word out*) Uh-uh! No! No! Not a word out of you! I'm *so sick* of setting something down and turning around to get it and it's gone! I'm putting together the entertainment center *you* had to have, and yes it has taken me a couple of days. I'm sorry! But if I leave the Phillips head out on the floor please leave...it...on...the...*floor*! *Not* in a utility drawer! *Not* back in my toolbox! *Not* up on a shelf so the neighbors don't see it when they drop by. God-Forbid! A *tool* lying on the floor! I draw the line here and today. You need to stop being a neat freak. (*Another example for Nancy comes to mind*) You know, when you put the toaster away this morning...yes...you *unplugged* the toaster and put it away while my *friggin' toast* was still in the toaster! I had to get it back out and finish toasting my bread. So you know what? (*Suddenly calms down and becomes quiet, contained anger*) You know what? I'm going to go get my Phillips head now. And wherever I place it that is where it will *stay* until I am done with your friggin' entertainment center, got it?

Alan from *Smashing the Pumpkins*
MALE about 60
DRAMATIC

Alan tells his local yet estranged brother Peter about the status of his son's health after a recent brutal attack.

Alan: Well, he was unconscious for nearly 14 days straight. He had a few seizures. He'll have permanent neurological deficits for the rest of his life. It's almost like he had a bad stroke. He'll keep having those seizures, he'll never speak the same, he's blind in his right eye, he can't walk without a cane...and his comprehension is extremely slow. Some things he can't understand at all. He watches Tom and Jerry cartoons all day long. He laughs at that show like he is eight years old all over again. It kills me Pete. It ain't right to see your boy grow up and get destroyed like that. George may not have been the most upright citizen. He never went to church or donated anything to charity. He never got a college degree or held a respectable job for more than two years. He may have had one too many drinks one too many times in his life, but my boy would never do that to a little girl. He has no reason, no motive, nothing. He was the closest suspect within proximity in that neighborhood and had no alibi. He's was a patsy.

Jake from *Patience of Hate*
MALE about 16-18
SERIO-COMIC

Jake tells his good friend about how sick he is of the hierarchy system in their school and the shallow ways that girls socialize with each other.

Jake: I'm sick of being "cute" to girls. They think *we're* shallow? No. I'm sick of the pettiness and the giggles. They're a bunch of back stabbing idiots. I just don't get it. I don't understand it. I like looking at them, but then they talk and ruin everything. Maybe it's high school. It's this place. Maybe it's the whole high school mentality. I dunno Lewis. I've just had it, it's frustrating. You never know what mood they're in, or what their stupid friends are going to tell them. They're so easily swayed by what the rest of the world thinks about them. Do you understand any of it? Then there's Helen. Her name is *Helen*. She's made fun of for being named Helen, she's made fun of for her mysterious illness. So what if she's sick and she's got this old-fashioned name? But she's the most beautiful person. And the "giggle girls" make fun of her. Making up diseases that she must have. Calling her Heinous Helen. She sits next to me in study hall, and she always says hello to me. She always asks me if I want a piece of gum. She doesn't send her annoying friends over to me to ask me if I think she's cute. She just smiles and ignores the rest of the world. I bet she's not sick at all. I bet everyone made up that crap to screw with her head.
(**Lewis:** She doesn't look too healthy these days.)
Jake: So what? I'll find out what's wrong with her. And whatever it is, I won't hold it against her, or spread rumors, or hate her for being different. And all of those other girls can piss off.

SCENES

Everyday Dribble
Maxine 25-40
Howard 25-40

A married couple argues over who is carrying more of a burden in their relationship.

Maxine: Do you know what would be wonderful?
Howard: If you left and never came back?
Maxine: Don't tempt me. No, you know what, while we're discussing perfection…it would be fabulous if you could just take your socks that you roll up into a ball and place *on* the lid of the hamper…if you could just lift the lid, now I know its an extra hand/arm motion, but if you could just lift the lid and just throw those socks in there, that would be great.
Howard: Yeah.
Maxine: Yeah?
Howard: What is the big deal?
Maxine: Exactly. What is the big deal about just lifting the lid and throwing the socks *into* the hamper?
Howard: Why do you have to make an issue out of it?
Maxine: No, no why do YOU have to make an issue out of it? It's simple to throw them into the hamper.
Howard: How about if I just throw them on the floor?
Maxine: You do that too.
Howard: Oh.
Maxine: And I don't really appreciate that either.
Howard: Yeah, what DO you appreciate?

Maxine: Um, you know I didn't even go into how you can't even take your socks off properly.
Howard: There is no proper way to take off socks.
Maxine: Look at them sometime! They're in balls! And usually - miraculously – half of them are in an inside-out ball shaped state. I don't even know how you do it! You are defying all the laws of physics by the very way you take off your socks.
Howard: Whatever.
Maxine: No, not whatever. DON'T "whatever" me. What are you? A teenaged girl? How much do you think I enjoy unrolling you stinky, crusty socks when I'm doing the laundry?
Howard: Why are you even talking about this?
Maxine: Why do I bother is more like it.
Howard: You have nothing else to do all day.
Maxine: Excuse me? So that's what all this attitude is about. You can't handle that I quit my job! I knew it! That's exactly when the sock balls started forming. What – you think I have daily picnics here? Can you even fathom how hard it is to pick up after you and the baby? On top of all the other things that need to get done?
Howard: Oh please. I didn't realize watching TV all day hurts your ass so much.
Maxine: Every easy, simple-minded, little thing you could do would make my life a little easier! How hard is it to flush the toilet when you're done?
Howard: You don't flush sometimes either.
Maxine: Only when I don't want to wake the baby, or when someone is in the shower. You do it everyday!
Howard: Oh please - -
Maxine: Not to mention, the dribble you leave on the rim, and the seat or lid is never down.
Howard: What is with you today?

Maxine: What do you do? Huh? You go in there, whip it out and piss all over and just walk out? It doesn't occur to you to put down the lid, or wipe up your dribbles or flush the freaking toilet?
Howard: (*Howard begins to stand up*) I'm out of here.
Maxine: Yeah, run away to you little cave. That'll really solve our problems...*your* problems.
Howard: (*Standing*) You are the one with the problems. I am perfectly happy with the way I conduct myself.
Maxine: Well, I would be too if someone else was picking up after me all the time.
Howard: What?
Maxine: Simple things! All I'm asking for is simple things! To show you care about all the big things that I do, to show you want to help out – even if it's a little! It feels like I do everything around the house.
Howard: Okay, how about I quit my job and you can go out and work all day. Full time.
Maxine: You really do think I sit around and watch TV all day don't you? You think I have it made, don't you? I have charity work; I have the fund drive at the hospital. Angelina alone is a handful. I deal with Angelina and she's always in need of something and...it's all work on top of other work. (*Exhausted, losing her fire*) Nevermind. I get it.
Howard: Get what?
Maxine: You. Your point.
Howard: What's my point?
Maxine: I do nothing all day and everyday, so I can just pick up after you...you'll give me something to do. Do you think the dishes do themselves? Dinner makes itself? The laundry folds itself up...after unrolling itself from tiny little balls...and places itself back into our drawers? The floors always sparkles, the toilets always shine and sinks are always spotless on their own?

Howard: And you wonder why things are the way they are.
Maxine: What do you mean by that?

Microwave beeps.

Howard: What are we having for dinner?
Maxine: Tacos. (*Pause*) How was work today?

The Ladies Room at Comet Cave
Andrea 21-30
Brynn 21-30

Two old friends talk about their growing disgust with the behavior of the people they associate themselves with.

Brynn sits alone in a chair in the Ladies Room. Andrea comes in.

Andrea: Alright Brynn, birthday girls don't mope in the bathroom. You should be happy; today's your day.
Brynn: I'm not stupid Andi.
Andrea: No one said you were.
Brynn: I know certain as sunshine that if I step one foot outside this ladies room, I'll be under the wrath of the Comet Cave Birthday Serenade. So - I'll be in this rest room facility until closing time.
Andrea: Johnny called off the "birthday serenade".
Byrnn: Please. You can't call those things off. Once it's out there, the song must be sung. The embarrassment must ensue. The birthday song sucks. It's got bad melody, it's got bad rhyme. No one can sing it in key. It almost becomes depressing if it's sung to slow. Anyway - I'm not moving from this spot.
Andrea: Something tells me something else is bothering you.
Brynn: Yep.
Andrea: Wanna talk about it?
Brynn: I don't even want to think about it. (*Pause*) But I'm going to anyway…so I may as well talk about it.
Andrea: Okay…
Brynn: Johnny had…he slept with…(*Makes a disgusted sound and grimaces*) Tammy.
Andrea: Yeah, so, who didn't?

Brynn: Yeah, but, eww... I mean...eww. Why him? Couldn't he refrain from a big ho like that? I mean he's so much better than that. He's smart, he's handsome, he's got personality - -

Andrea: And he's a *guy*. Was he lying to you about it?

Brynn: No, he doesn't know that I know. Trixie told me. (*Really fixed on 'Tammy' thoughts*) But Tammy? C'mon! Her name is Tammy! That's your first sign! All girls named Tammy are sluts...this is common knowledge!

Andrea: I'm pretty sure all girls named Tracy are skanks too.

Brynn: Andi, eww...I don't think I can fall in love with a guy who sunk so low as to sleep with Tammy Hill.

Andrea: If it makes you feel any better, I know a lot of guys she slept with.

Brynn: That's just the point.

Andrea: Oh, right.

Brynn: Plus - he slept with Liz...and Veronica.

Andrea: Veronica? Veronica the - -

Brynn: The bartender, yup. You bet.

Andrea: Liz is here too.

Brynn: (*Getting angry*) Yup – the whole gang is here! It's like a club! Wanna join? All you have to do is...Johnny...its too bad you're not a big ho, you probably already would've.

Andrea: So dump him.

Brynn: I can't.

Andrea: Why?

Brynn: I think I really like him.

Andrea: Well, you'll get over this. Time will heal.

Brynn: Why do we always have to come here? With all his ex-conquests? Everywhere I turn there's another one starring me right in the face. And you know what? Its not that I'm jealous of them. I mean, Tammy? Please. I couldn't be jealous of her if I was a garbage bag. I just feel so unimportant to him. I guess that's what it is.

Andrea: At least you don't feel like you're dating your brother.

Brynn: Still with Mike, huh?

Andrea: He's really sweet. And we have so much in common. I just feel like I'm kissing my brother.

Brynn: Ugh.

Andrea: I know. Mike just feels all wrong in a physical way. I mean I'm attracted to him and as soon as things get physical, it just feels wrong.

Brynn: Take some of your advice, dump him.

Andrea: I can't.

Brynn: Why?

Andrea: Because, he's clean, organized, gorgeous...motivated. He told me when he gets married and his wife gets pregnant he has a list of things he wants the doctor to check so he's sure the mom and baby are all okay. What guy says that? He's a gem! He doesn't do drugs like all those other creeps. We like the same TV shows, the same movies. He's as into *Celebrities Uncensored* as I am! How many guys do you know like that?

Brynn: Did he have sex with Tammy?

Andrea: I don't think he knows Tammy.

Brynn: Count your blessings. Is he coming tonight?

Andrea: No, he's working. I just don't know what to do about the sibling feeling I have toward him.

Brynn: You guys have too much in common.

Andrea: What?

Brynn: Opposites attract and he's exactly like you - into the same things as you. It's like your dating the male version of you. That's why he feels like a brother to you.

Andrea: I guess that makes sense, huh?

Brynn: You have to find a way to make that brotherly feeling toward him turn into something romantic and you'll get over it.
Andrea: (*Thoughtful*) Huh...
Brynn: Okay now solve my problem.
Andrea: How to make incest romantic? Hmmm...
Brynn: Back to me here! Focus! My problem takes priority due to its immediate nature.
Andrea: Okay. You should -
Brynn: Kill Tammy.
Andrea: Killing Tammy won't solve your problem. You need to talk to Johnny.
Brynn: Happy flippin' birthday to me.

Everything Pink
Beth Ann 35-45
Hank about 22

A married couple have a morning "conversation."

Beth Ann: Good mornin' handsome.
Hank: It's mornin'. It ain't so good.
Beth Ann: If the good Lord has you wake up each day, it's a sign he wants you to go on.
Hank: (*In unison*) it's a sign he wants you to go on. You and the Lord.
Beth Ann: Did you sleep well?
Hank: Yalp. Could keep on sleepin'. *(Plops down on the couch)*
Beth Ann: (*Pause*) Lovely collection of toe nails you left there on the couch for me.
Hank: Them were beauties.
Beth Ann: On a scale of one to ten, how difficult is it to walk ten paces to that there garbage can and toss them out?
Hank: I forgot.
Beth Ann: Please try to remember from now on. It took everything I had not to gag.
Hank: Please, they're toenails. Not lower intestines.
Beth Ann: It's all gross just the same. Hank, you need to get dressed and eat. Honey Ann is comin' to visit today.
Hank: What's she want?
Beth Ann: She's our daughter. I think she just wants to visit us. It's her first visit since she moved out.
Hank: She's *your* daughter.
Beth Ann: She's like a daughter to you.
Hank: If you say so.
Beth Ann: Just get yourself ready for company.

Hank: Right now?
Beth Ann: Yes. Now get. (*Coughs and hold her crotch*)
Hank: Thought you quit smoking.
Beth Ann: I did. I still cough.
Hank: What's with the cigarette?
Beth Ann: I bought a pack just to hold.
Hank: To hold?
Beth Ann: I miss holdin' um. I miss the smell. I'm not smoking um. (*Coughs and holds her crotch*)
Hank: Gotta pee?
Beth Ann: I'm old, I had children, my bladder is…just go make yourself somewhat presentable.
Hank: (*As he's exiting stage*) I still don't see the big deal; she lived here with us for years for Christopher's sake.
Beth Ann: (*Puts toe nails in Hank's cereal box, audience may or may not know what she's up to*) The Lord's name is only used in good reference in this house.
Hank: (*Off stage*) Christopher ain't the Lord's name. And this ain't no house.
Beth Ann: (*Takes off her ratty old robe*) Trailer. And the insinuation behind "Christopher" is the Lord's name.
Hank: (*Off stage*) Ooo… "insinuation." Showing off your new vocabulary? (*Pause*) Where's my nice plain white polo shirt?
Beth Ann: In the closet. And I happen to know the word "insinuation" without the help of my word-a-day vocabulary calendar.
Hank: You hung it up?
Beth Ann: My calendar?
Hank: No, dang it, the shirt! You hung it up?
Beth Ann: Well, it's your best one, Hank. Why don't you wear that nice button-up shirt your mamma sent for Christmas?

Hank: It's too hot. That polister gives me B.O.
Beth Ann: You mean polyester?
Hank: Whatever, its makes me stink.
Beth Ann: Are you almost ready? I don't wanna be horsin' around when Honey Ann gets here.
Hank: What you invite her over so early for?
Beth Ann: It's almost one in the afternoon.
Hank: I'm almost done.
Beth Ann: Well hurry on up, we ain't got all day!

Abandon and Illness
Generic scene for both age and gender.

A couple of old friends try to mend their estrangement.

A: What are you doing here?
B: I came to see you.
A: (*pause*) Now? Why now?
B: You're sick and I - I haven't...honestly...I haven't been a very good friend.
A: Oh really? Did that just occur to you? Because I started to figure it out after you didn't return my last half a dozen calls over the past year.
B: I'm so sorry, I never meant neglect you like that.
A: Well you did. And now it's done. You can leave now.
B: I don't want to leave. I came here to make things right.
A: You don't even want to be here in the first place. You're only here out of guilt... or on a dare... or maybe someone paid to you come here.
B: Please... I just... I've been in denial. Part of me didn't want to talk to you, because I didn't want to face the reality.
A: Part of you? Part of you didn't want to talk to me and face *my* reality? What did the other part of you want? Not to be *bothered* with my reality? And what about me? I'm out here facing the tests and the chemo... and the one person who I thought I could lean on in the bad times just disappears? (*Disgusted*) Get out of here; I can't stand to look at you.
B: Please don't. Don't dismiss this.
A: You're the one who dismissed this every time you didn't call me back. Or return my e-mails. Or send me

a birthday card. Don't try to pile this guilt on me. I'm carrying enough of a weight.

B: I'm here to try and carry some of that weight with you. I should have been there for you before. Don't you think I know that?

A: I don't know what I think about you anymore. (*Beat*) I thought I knew you... and I thought I could rely on you. And it broke my heart – the moment I needed you most...the moment I thought I could lean on you for support and you abandoned me.

B: I realize that it was wrong. Do you know how hard it was for me to come here today? Do you know how stupid and horrible I feel? Please... we've been through so much, and I had very poor judgment. I'm so sorry.

A: (*Considering*) Honestly, right now - I'm just too sick to hold grudges. But I'm not going to be too quick to forgive this either. You really hurt me.

B: I know. It kills me to hear you say that, but I understand. I just hope that me being here now proves something...

A: The sincerity in your eyes says something. Just... promise me right now that you won't do that to me again. Please.

B: I promise. I'm here...I'm not going anywhere.

For a Good Cause
Generic scene for both age and gender.

In an office setting a solicitor approaches the head of a company for a holiday donation.

Solicitor: (*Rings a loud bell several times*) Good afternoon sir/ma'am!
CEO: How on earth did you get in here?
Solicitor: No one was at the front desk. I just came right in.
CEO: (*Looks down, dismissing*) Please find your way out.
Solicitor: Just one moment of your time... I was wondering if you would be so kind as to give a small charitable donation to our cause we - -
CEO: And *I* was wondering if you noticed the plaque on our main office door that clearly states "no soliciting".
Solicitor: I noticed it.
CEO: Do you know what soliciting is?
Solicitor: Yes, it is generally defined as a request or plea... However, I am kindly *asking* you for a donation. Anything you can give will be deeply appreciated.
CEO: Asking, requesting, pleading... it's all soliciting, which is not allowed in here.
Solicitor: And may I ask who made up this rule?
CEO: No!
Solicitor: You're the Chief Executive Officer here, right? Aren't you the one who makes up the rules?
CEO: The rules are company policies. They are what they are and they will be enforced! Please find your way out or I will call security to personally escort you out.
Solicitor: Hold on, hold on... I stand outside of these offices every day - and you pass me by in the morning, and you pass me by in the afternoon... I just thought I'd

come in here to save you the hassle of digging around for change in the cold - -

CEO: (*Interrupting*) How very thoughtful of you. (*Beat*) Please leave.

Solicitor: Just hear me out...

CEO: I'm picking up the phone now...

Solicitor: (*Gets angry and loud*) HEY! Enough with the threats! (*Beat*) I'm coming to you in a time of need! You are a CEO of a huge corporation. I don't know what you do here, but you drive a nice car, you wear nice clothes, and you walk the walk... it bugs the heck out of me that you can't throw in a quarter every now and again! (*Beat*) I ring my bell the loudest when you walk by!

CEO: (*Interrupting the rant*) Thank you – yes - I've noticed.

Solicitor: Good! So stop being such a stingy jerk and cough up a few coins for the less fortunate!

CEO: (*Beat*) Will a few candies do? (*Pushes the candy dish on his/her desk toward the Solicitor*)

Solicitor: No!

CEO: Fine. (*Digs in pocket and produces some change*) Here.

Solicitor looks at the meager donation in his/her basket, clears his/her throat and shoves the basket in the CEO's face. CEO gives a slightly annoyed sigh and places a few bills or coins in the basket.

CEO: No one ever finds out about this. (*Beat*) I have a stingy reputation to maintain around here.

Solicitor: Your secret is safe with me.

CEO: Get out of here.

Solicitor: While I'm at it there was one other issue I wanted to - -

CEO: OUT!

Solicitor: I'm out; I'm out! Thank you and Happy Holidays!!! (*Exits ringing the obnoxious bell*)

Spats
Veronica 13-16
Alicia 13-16

Two girls have a disagreement about secrecy and trust in a school cafeteria.

Veronica and Alicia just sit down at the lunch table at school. Veronica is quieter than usual and Alicia attempts to ignore Veronica's mood at first, but things get to the point where the "mood" can't be ignored.

Alicia: I'm getting so sick of these peanut butter and jelly sandwiches. They put way too much peanut butter on these things.
Veronica: *(Quiet)* So get something else.
Alicia: This *is* my something else. It's the only alternative to the other garbage they insist on serving. How can any of this food be considered healthy? It's all like flavored cardboard.
Veronica: *(Quieter)* Yeah.
Alicia: *(Debating at first)* What's up with you today, Ron? You were quiet in gym, you're barely eating anything… are you sick?
Veronica: No.
Alicia: Well what is it then? You're not yourself.
Veronica: I'm fine.
Alicia: No you're not.
Veronica: *(Pause)* Alicia, I know what you did.
Alicia: What'd I do?
Veronica: Don't act like you don't know what I'm talking about.
Alicia: Honestly, I have no idea.
Veronica: I found out from Kaleigh that she heard that I have a thing for Justin Pearce.

Alicia: Really?

Veronica: Yes... really. How on earth would Kaleigh know about that?

Alicia: I have no idea.

Veronica: I think you do. You are the only person I told about that.

Alicia: I didn't tell anyone, I promised I wouldn't. You must have told someone else.

Veronica: I didn't.

Alicia: Well, Kaleigh won't tell anyone - -

Veronica: *(Interrupting)* Kaleigh has the biggest mouth out of anyone I know! I never would have told her... look, the only person I told was you. And now, this is going to get back to Justin.

Alicia: Is that a bad thing?

Veronica: Yes, that's a bad thing. Look, that's not even the point right now, the point is – I trusted you. And you blabbed.

Alicia: I swear I didn't.

Veronica: Liar.

Alicia: Ronnie, I didn't... if I did it was totally by accident - -

Veronica: *If* you did? What? Do you have some sort of memory loss now? It's simple Alicia, I asked you not to tell anyone and you opened *your* big mouth to *biggest* mouth in this school. How can I possibly confide in you about anything from now on?

Alicia: I'm sorry.

Veronica: So you blabbed.

Alicia: I didn't do it to be vicious. I just know that Kaleigh knows Justin really well - -

Veronica: Exactly!

Alicia: ...and I thought she might have some sort of an "in" with Justin that would benefit you.

Veronica: Next time let me be the judge of that.

Alicia: I'm really sorry.

Am I Evil? Yes I Am
Zoe Pratt – Patron, 22-40
Bartender – Male or female, any age

Zoe discusses her inner struggle with whether or not she is a good person.

Bartender: *(Drying a glass with a dish towel)* Does this always bother you?
Zoe: You have no idea.
Bartender: You're this conflicted about your own intentions?
Zoe: What does it mean?
Bartender: Tell me more. Tell me about the panic attacks.
Zoe: I can control them now. Thank God.
Bartender: When did they start?
Zoe: I was twelve. My father said to me, "When you're 80, I certainly won't be around anymore."
Bartender: That triggered it?
Zoe: Yeah. I finally thought about life having a true end. A true black end. Nothing left…no parents…never seeing anyone again. Not waking up ever again. Everything gone – just as it was before my birth. The words, "It's really going to happen," just kept repeating over and over in my head. And I got sucked into this vortex…is that the right word?
Bartender: If you're referring to a catastrophic whirlwind of power…yes.
Zoe: That works. Every time I'd think about it I'd get sucked into that vortex. And do you know the scariest thing about that?
Bartender: What?

Zoe: Nothing in this world feels more real to me than *that* fear. I felt as though I discovered a pure truth in those panic attacks.

Bartender: Fear can give you a rush Zoe. That rush can bring an element of reality that isn't necessarily a truth…but more of an altered level of living.

Zoe: Well – it left a deep impression.

Bartender: Are you spiritual?

Zoe: I don't know what to think. I suppose I am. Are you?

Bartender: Yea. Doesn't that bring you a degree of comfort?

Zoe: Possibly. It may be the reason why I don't have the panic attacks anymore.

Bartender: If you don't have the panic attacks anymore…then what's the problem?

Zoe: I…I think I'm evil.

Bartender: Evil? What makes you think that?

Zoe: Well for starters, my husband can't resist when kids sell items door to door.

Bartender: (*pause*) I don't follow…

Zoe: There's more…Okay - he bought a newspaper subscription from a little girl. Not just Sundays…or Thursdays through Sundays, no – the *whole* bloomin' week. Which just makes more work for me. And it's for a whole year! We won't read them, we'll waste our money, and it'll be one more thing cluttering up the house. Couldn't we just give the little girl a $20 and tell her to get lost?

Bartender: And you believe that that makes you evil?

Zoe: I'm not a good person when I'm stressed. And I hate when I'm that person. I hate when I'm too busy to concentrate on my son's latest colored picture.

Bartender: It's perfectly natural to doubt your parenting skills.

Zoe: I can't stand the sound of him chewing anymore.

Bartender: What?
Zoe: I hate the sound of him chewing.
Bartender: Who?
Zoe: My husband. It drives me crazy. Especially corn on the cob. I'm insane with crazy when he chews. I hate it.
Bartender: Maybe this is more about your marriage than anything else. How long have you been married?
Zoe: No, it's not just my marriage. I cheer for people when they are set back, I secretly jeer for them when they excel. I like people's misfortune to make me feel better about my life. I despise the success of others because it makes my life seem worthless and pointless.
Bartender: That can be very natural Zoe, many people -
Zoe: Everyone is prettier, smarter, and better than I am.
Bartender: Zoe, how often do you feel like this?
Zoe: Which is worse? Lying to someone and telling them you think they'll do great when you know failure is inevitable? Or just being honest about it and saying, 'You will fail.'
Bartender: White lies at the expense of harmless positive reinforcement toward others are usually the way to go.
Zoe: Do all negative thoughts make me a bad person? Why can't I feel genuine happiness for someone when they achieve something great…why is it always envy or jealousy?
Bartender: All of this makes you feel as though you are evil?
Zoe: Yes. I think I really am.
Bartender: How often to you reflect on these behavior traits of yours?
Zoe: I sometimes wonder…they have ridiculously dumb shows about weddings, dating, make-overs, baby stories…what about divorce, custody battles, diseases and death stories?

Bartender: That's called the news. Although, I'm sure if you'd start a Goth Channel those shows would be a great pitch. *(Pause)* Zoe, I think you're over analyzing yourself. You're human. We all have these thoughts cross our minds. But they are only thoughts. You have the choice to re-think your reaction and you have the choice to do and say the right thing…which I'm sure you usually do. Let me ask you this…if your friend lost a child to an early death – would that tragedy really make you happy?
Zoe: God. No. But I don't think I'd feel as badly as I should. There would still be a shred in me that was thankful that it wasn't me going through that.
Bartender: Feeling genuinely happy about a horrible situation that another is going through is evil. To be thankful for what you have and don't have is actually healthy. To say to someone, "Thank goodness I'm not going through your spiraling hell" would be evil… to say, "I'm so sorry you're going through that," would be more appropriate… and I'm sure that's what you'd do.

There is a pause as Zoe contemplates this possibility.

Zoe: What do you think about before you know you're about to die? What if you have no time to think? What if you can't think anymore and you've long lost your mind? Do you think about your regrets? Do you think about your fear? Do you wish you had more children? Do you think about God? Do you doubt in your God? Do you tell anyone what you're really thinking? Do you wish you loved more?
Bartender: I'm sure it's different from person to person.
Zoe: It is the bravest thing that all of us must do.
Bartender: It isn't bravery really – is it? Death is an unavoidable event. We all must do it – brave or not.

Zoe: Are you trying to push me back into that vortex?

Bartender: You brought it up again. So I must ask again, doesn't your spirituality bring you a form of comfort?

Zoe: My spiritual world relies and lives in the fact that all things cannot be explained. You know, my grandmother recently passed away, I didn't find myself all that sad. Doesn't that sound harsh? I was really close with her growing up. Then - I realized it is because I *knew* I'd see her again. I just knew that. I have faith in that feeling. That is where my spirituality lies. We must have faith in all the things that cannot be explained. And that is my religion.

Bartender: That doesn't sound evil to me.

Zoe: I don't know. Why don't we bond with other people anymore? Strangers? Why don't we look at anyone in the eye anymore? Why don't we really pay attention to the smaller moments? You know - the moments that are just there everyday, but we take advantage of them? Can't we get over ourselves and just see the world for its constant beauty? Maybe. Maybe. I know why we don't look anyone in the eye. I know why we take advantage of the smaller things, and let our busy lives constantly consume our every thought. It's because if we did realize how lucky we are to have right now, we'd break down. Because deep down – we all know it won't last. It's the beauty of life that holds me down. The beauty holds us all down and forces us to be evil – because the beauty would break our hearts.

Bartender: I'm not sure I follow...

Zoe: I'm on a rant here, please keep up. Were we as humans ever supposed to evolve into conscious beings? Are we doomed to question the purpose of our existence – is that the price we pay as conscious beings? Intelligent beings?

Bartender waits to see if it's okay for her to speak.

Zoe: Well?
Bartender: My God, which one do you want me to answer? Look, Zoe, you make some valid points and you ask some thought provoking questions, but you need to search yourself. You ultimately need to answer your questions. For now, you need to take what you know to be true about your life, and what you believe through speculation and run with it. Time will change your perspective, but understand… you will never have all of the answers. And some of your answers may be wrong. But everything you know and believe will give you a basis to live your life in some form of peace. And that's all we can ask for in this life.
Zoe: (*Thoughtful for a moment*) Thanks. (*Beat*) I better go.
Bartender: (*Looks at watch*) I'll see you next week?
Zoe: Probably. (*Gets up to leave*) Thank you.
Bartender: Zoe, are you still – honestly - convinced that you're evil?
Zoe: Yes I am.

ONE ACT PLAYS

On Candleswick Avenue

Sarah – female, mid-twenties
Angel Thealius – male, any age
Jim – male, any age

Sarah is stuck in purgatory with Angel Thealius.

Sarah is somewhat disoriented and walks to DC to meet up with Angel.

Sarah: Are you God?
Angel: No.
Sarah: Who are you? Where am I?
Angel: I'm a like…an administrative assistant…You are on Candleswick Avenue. If you look down you can see the accident you just had.
Sarah: *(Looking down)* Wow.
Angel: *(Looking down too)* Yea, wasn't even your fault.
Sarah: *(Looks back at Angel)* Candleswick Avenue?
Angel: Yea, you need to blow out your candle. *(Points in the direction of a lit candle)*
Sarah: This isn't heaven?
Angel: It's the gates…you need to blow out your candle. And then – see that pretty light over there? *(points)* We walk over there and…wallah! Heaven.
Sarah: You mean my life is over?
Angel: 'Fraid so.
Sarah: Where's God?

Angel: God is busy. You'll have to settle for me. (Looking at clipboard) You have an appointment with God in two weeks…

Sarah: But I'm too young. There must be a mistake.

Angel: Yea, uh – you were going to be what (looking at papers on clip board)…27 next week…aw jeez…just before the birthday. Well, look - young people die all the time. Most of them have no choice.

Sarah: So I have a choice?

Angel: No! *(Laughs a little)* No, no – only a very few exceptions are made…so just come this way…see- see the pretty light? *(Points again)*

Sarah: *(Gives it a quick glance)* It's not all that pretty.

Angel: Sure it is just look at it – pure beauty resonating all around you… it wants to embrace you.

Sarah: No. It doesn't seem right.

Angel: Look God says it's your time. You are needed. And the light…(*Tries to make it sound irresistible*)

Sarah: The light is not interesting me in the least.

Angel: You didn't even look at it! Just look at the friggin' light! *(Angel goes over and forces Sarah to look directly at the light)*.

Sarah: *(Falling into a daze looking at it)* Oooo…it is very pretty. Is that glitter? I just need to touch it a little…(*She slowly walks toward it, stops, shakes her head and snaps out of the trance*). No, no…it just isn't right. I was driving my car…it wasn't my fault… *(Turns to look at Angel)* None of this feels right. Are you're smoking?

Angel: I'm a little stressed out here. It's a dry ice… nothing but dry ice… it's very good for the lungs. Especially in my case – where I don't have any lungs. Back to the light…we really should catch that train before it passes us by.

Sarah: *(Looking down at the accident)* Look at me. I look horrible. But I need to go back. I need to go on.

Angel: Hey – you don't want to go back to that body. Here come the medics.
Sarah: Am I still breathing?
Angel: No. (*Gives a quick second look*) Well, maybe a little.
Sarah: I want to go back. I need to go back. Please make an exception. I didn't get to say 'goodbye'.
Angel: You don't get to say goodbye. (*Sees Sarah is not at all comforted by Angels words*) Look, (*Grabs the folder file with Sarah's name on it*) your mom and dad are at home watching the game and in 12 minutes they are going to get the call that you were in an accident and you passed on in the ambulance on the way to the hospital - -
Sarah: There is time! Please send me back.
Angel: I can't undo God's will.
Sarah: Why does God need me so badly?
Angel: (*Very polite and calm*) Hold on. (*Gets out a mobil phone and speaks in to the phone*) Yeah, I got a 34-11 here. Twenty-six years old, broadside in time zone 22...that's the one...Sarah...(*Whispers*) She's not responding to the light...c'mon! I need a teleport here in two minutes, two minutes – it's a stinkin' 34-11! Thank you...(*Hangs up*) jackass. So what's your story...why aren't you responding to the light?
Sarah: I really want to go back. I want to have a husband and children.... I barely had a chance to live at all... what's your name?
Angel: Thealius.
Sarah: Thealius, do you...or *did* you have a wife and kids?
Angel: Yes. But they're all here now...in fact I always look down on my Great-Great-Grandchildren...oh.
Sarah: I will have no one to look down on. When my parents join me here...I'll have nothing left. I was a fairly decent person please let me go back...

Jim enters.

Jim: Okay gang…what seems to be the bother?
Angel: Hi Jim…this one wants to go back…
Jim: Not interested in the light?
Angel: Nope.
Jim: What's your name sweetie?
Sarah: Sarah. Uh…who are you?
Jim: Did you see the pretty light over there? It's God calling upon you…God wants you to be a part of his kingdom…
Angel: She's not interested.
Sarah: I'm too young. I have so much I want to do with my life.
Angel: She's a motivated one.
Sarah: Please – make an exception and send me back.
Jim: I'm sorry, the will of God is done – there are no exceptions.
Sarah: But, Thealius said exceptions have been made.
Jim: Oh, really? Thealius, can I have a word with you?

Jim and Thealius pull off to the side and you can hear bickering – Jim is annoyed at Thealius and Thealius is a bit defensive and apologetic. No exact words are understood. Sarah is looking down at the accident. They stop bickering and return to where they were.

Jim: (*Looking down at accident*) That doesn't look so bad. (*To Angel Thealius*) Was this a punishment thing? (*To Sarah*) What did you do that was so wrong?
Sarah: Wrong? Nothing. I mean…I was human… occasionally dishonest, greedy, and selfish. I seriously contemplated posing nude for a while.
Jim and Angel: (*In counterpoint*) Oh, nothing wrong with that. No, don't see the harm done there.
Jim: Anyway, you didn't murder anyone?

Angel: No.

Sarah shakes her head

Jim: Cheat on the husband?
Angel: Not married.
Jim: Do you want to go to heaven?
Sarah: Someday – not today.
Jim: Let me see the file (*Takes it from Angel*) Uh-huh…oh…interesting…did you see this?

Showing something to Angel

Angel: How 'bout that? Don't see many of those up here…
Sarah: What are you guys looking at? (*They start quietly laughing*) What are you laughing at?
Jim: (*Clears his throat and gets serious*) Nothing, nothing…uh, okay Miss Sarah, I'll need you to sign here and here. We can release you to your former physical self for a period of…
Sarah: Wait! Don't tell me when I'm going to die!
Angel: Alright, but be aware that next time we're chopping you up into little pieces so we don't have this situation again.
Jim: Don't tell her that! He's kidding. Now – be aware – your leg has been broken and a rib is cracked. Your lawsuit will be just enough to cover a new car and that nose job you've been wanting since eighth grade.
Sarah: Really?
Angel: Just be aware – God frowns upon alterations of holy creations, but forgives you.
Jim: Any who – you have ten days to change your mind at which time you can take your own life with no punishment or purgatory. We'll grant you heaven within the ten days only. After that point in time you must wait

for natural death or murder to take you.
Sarah: Why would I want to take my life within the next ten days?
Angel: After seeing the light and feeling the presence of heaven, when you return to your mortal self you will be tempted to come back to this carefree, painless world…and it may be too much to take. It's all just a precaution.
Jim: God understands.
Angel: And forgives.
Sarah: I will not be in any hurry to come back here…I like living.
Angel: Good enough…. just sign here.

Sarah signs

Jim: And just pass through that black hole over there and you'll shortly be sucked back into your old body. You …uh…won't remember any of this.
Sarah: That's fine.
Jim: Except the light. It's hard for us to erase the light. You just might remember the light.
Angel: Most people do.
Sarah: Thank you so much! (*Walks away*)
Jim: (*Both watch her disappear*) Oooo…that's *gotta* hurt. (*To Angel Thealius*) You always get the sticklers.
Angel: The light is supposed to do all the work! I don't get it…
Jim: Come on, you owe me a beer….

Lights down

In the Swing Line

Stapler – male or female, any age
Jenna – female, 20-30s
Jenna's boss – male or female, any age

A stapler comes to life and asks Jenna to give him/her some respect.

Lights up on Jenna is sitting at her desk slamming the stapler at her desk. Lights come up on Stapler looking at Jenna slam her stapler. When Stapler talks, Jenna will eventually focus only on the Stapler, but the actor playing the Stapler will stand off the side in a spotlight acting out the lines.

Stapler: Whoa, whoa! Easy! Easy!

Jenna looks around suspiciously. She looks behind her. She slams a few more papers.

Stapler: Enough already!
Jenna: What? (*Looking around*)
Stapler: Is the rough banging necessary? I' mean – if you're pissed off or something, fine, but don't take to out on me.
Jenna: (*Still looking around*) I – I'm not pissed off. I'm just stapling.
Stapler: *Just* stapling? No, no no… you are in demolition mode. Nothing will be left of me if you go on like this…
Jenna: Nothing will be left of - -
Stapler: Look at me when I'm talking to you!

Jenna looks at the stapler.

Stapler: That's right. That's better.

Jenna picks up the stapler.

Stapler: Don't – don't pick me up! No! Put me down this instant!

Jenna opens the loading section of the stapler.

Stapler: Put that down right now… close that! Inappropriate! This is not the time for that!

Jenna puts the stapler down in the center of the desk.

Stapler: Thank you. Now… just focus on me… all your attention on the stapler. (*Jenna attempts to touch the stapler*) *Don't!* Don't touch me! Just *listen* to me… Look, I am your saving grace. I hold together all of those important papers that need grouping and separation. I have a very important job – and you slamming away at me isn't healthy for either of us. Think about all of the carpal tunnel possibilities.
Jenna: I really don't feel as though I was…hurting you. After all, you are just a stapler.
Stapler: Awww… there it is. I knew that was coming. *Just a stapler.* Well you're *just* an administrative assistant. There. I said it. Bang. (*Beat*) For your information, I am the most reliable piece of equipment here on your desk and you know it. You'd be lost without me.
Jenna: I wouldn't call you reliable. You do unexpectedly run out of staples.
Stapler: Only when you're not on top of my staple supply. That's your job, not mine. I'm just the stapler… I pull through on my end of the bargain.

Jenna: Well...I guess. But paper clips give me just as much freedom and satisfaction.
Stapler: Please. A paper clip doesn't have what I got. And a paper clip could never satisfy you the way that I do - and you know it.
Jenna: They separate and group properly *and* without the commitment of two holes piercing the corner of my papers.
Stapler: Look, paper clips are crap. They slip off, they cause indentations and occasional rips in the papers... they're nothing but trouble. Don't tell them I told you this, but they tangle up together in that bin just to piss you off. They all laugh about it after hours. I heard them.
Jenna: Well...the tape works just fine...
Stapler: Awww...*tape*? How often do you use *tape*? C'mon! The tape dispenser is on the fritz too. And then there are those jaws of death that un-do all of my hard work.
Jenna: The staple-pull?
Stapler: That's what's they're calling that death instrument? (*Jenna nods*) Did you know they sold that thing with me? Like we're friends or something. And we match! The same color... it's sickening.
Jenna: I'll just put that in my drawer if it bothers you.
Stapler: Yes, please. I'd appreciate that. (*Beat*) And that pen caddy is just unstable.
Jenna: Well, my computer - -
Stapler: DON'T even get me *started* on that box of STDs. That thing is the most untrustworthy thing here. I'm ashamed to share a desk with it. (*Hushed*) Don't tell it I told you that please... he's got access to a lot of information... it's kinda scary.
Jenna: (*Sighs*) I suppose you are the most reliable thing here. The phone is nothing but a disturbance, the scissors are bulky and dull, the pens blotch and don't

write the way I want them to, and even the drawers on this desk don't slide freely – the handle is half off on this one drawer. (*Beat*) You *are* a gem compared to everything else here. You *are* reliable. I haven't appreciated all the things that you do… and I'm so sorry.
Stapler: Look, let's be honest here. I'm a stapler. I'm not asking much… you don't have to say thank you every time I successfully drive metal through your designated groups of papers. All I ask is… take it easy lady. You have one mean, forceful fist and I don't like to be on the receiving end of that. It's not cool.
Jenna: (*Jenna's boss walks in unknown to her*) I'm sorry stapler. I promise to be more careful from now on. (*Pets the stapler*) And even if I don't always say it… thank you for always being there, being reliable, and doing your job. It makes my job easier, and I appreciate that. Thank you stapler. Thank you.
Jenna's boss: Good morning, Jenna.
Jenna: 'Morning.
Jenna's boss: Everything okay?
Jenna: Yes, absolutely.
Jenna's boss: (*Walks away*) Very good then.
Jenna: (*Sinks behind her desk*) Yeah.

GLOSSARY
General Acting Terms

This glossary of terms is very basic and serves to help those who are new or just starting to dabble in the world of stage and theatre acting. These words are key terms used frequently when you're part of a production. While some of these terms are used in film and television, most of them are more commonly applied in theatre.

Acting Area (a.k.a. "Stage" or "Playing Area") – The playing area for the actors and set where the audience can be in full view of the performance.

Actor – One who acts in plays or a performance and portrays one or more characters.

AFTRA – American Federation of Television and Radio Artists.

Artistic Director - Normally in charge of the programming of a venue and might also direct the shows.

Assistant Director – Assists the director with notes, errands, and random duties.

Audition – The process of an actor showing the casting director of a production what they can do. Actors are sometimes asked to memorize a relevant monologue they'd like to perform for the director. More often than not, an actor will be asked to do a "Cold Reading" which tests the actor's response to a piece of text that they have not prepared to read.

Background – "Extra" performers often used to create a crowd.

Backstage – The area where the audience cannot see and actors can have costume changes, and props stored.

Beat – An intentional pause for dramatic or comedic effect.

Black Box – A type of intimate, nontraditional, flexible, studio theatre space that both the audience and the performers share.

Blocking – The staging of actors in required positions for a scene. All movements are generally noted and recorded within the acting area. Sometimes there are tape markers for precise placing.

Call Back - A second or subsequent audition for actors as the auditors narrow down the pool of potential actors for their production.

Call Time – The time that an actor is due to be on set for a performance.

Calling the Show – Usually done by the stage manager, this is the process of calling all of the verbal cues for sound, lighting, stage crew, scenery changes, etc.

Cast – The complete group of actors who perform within a given script, play or film.

Casting - The procedure of the director selecting the actors to perform the characters in the script.

Center – Center of the stage.

Cold Read – When an actor is given a limited amount of time before reading a portion of the script "cold" in front of an audition panel.

Costume – Prearranged outfit(s) worn by the actors in the performance.

Costume Designer – Person who chooses proper attire for each specific character while keeping in mind the style during that particular time period within the script.

Curtain Call – The very end of the performance when the entire cast comes out on stage to take a bow and acknowledge the audience's applause.

Curtain Speech - Introduction just before the performance starts which is generally given by the director or theatre owner (etc.) from the stage. Sometimes this can be replaced with a recorded announcement: "Good Evening Ladies and Gentlemen and welcome to the (insert name) Theatre. May I remind you to please turn off your cell phones. We hope you enjoy the show!"

Dailies – Viewing footage before it is edited.

Dialogue – Discussions and exchanges between characters on stage.

Director – There are many types of directors within a production. Generally speaking, the role of a director encompasses being responsible for the complete artistic vision of a production.

Downstage – Closest to audience.

Dress Rehearsal – A full run of a script with all technical elements involved; private practice for a public performance.

Dressing Rooms – Designated rooms for actors that store costumes, provide a changing space, and furnish mirrors.

Ensemble – A group production of supporting players.

Executive Director – The administrative manager in charge of the venue.

Extra – An actor who has no speaking role, but becomes part of the background or crowd.

Fourth Wall – The imaginary wall where the audience views the performance.

Headshot – A professional photo that accurately depicts the best of an actor's facial physical attributes. The name of the actor is printed across the bottom of the photo and sometimes there is a resume printed on the back.

House – The audience or the seating are of the audience.

House Lights – The lighting for the audience to see their way to their seats as well as in the vestibule area.

Intermission – The break (generally 10 to 20 minutes in duration) between acts during a performance.

Lead Role – The main role in the piece.

Left Stage – Actors left when facing the audience.

Lighting Designer – (LD) Part of the production team who is responsible for the overall look and effect of the lighting in the performance. They are responsible for communicating with the director about the overall style and with the set and costume designers about color.

Make-up – Coloring and powder products applied to the face to enhance or evoke a certain look.

Monologue – A speech given by an actor who may or may not be alone on stage.

Notes – A list of alterations, omissions, and improvements from the director that are shared with all of the cast (or only specific actors) after a rehearsal or performance to revise and make improvements on the show.

On Book – Someone who is "on book" reads along over the text of a scene (or monologue) *while* an actor does the scene. If the actor forgets the lines, the person "on book" can help along the actor by taking over and reading a few words to refresh the actor's memory. The actor doesn't break character, but only says "line" to request his or her lines.

Off Book – When all dialogue/lines are memorized by the actor.

Off Stage – Anything out of the view of the audience; generally speaking, it is off to the sides and back stage.

Pit – The area where the orchestra plays, practices, and houses their instruments.

Places – A call from the stage manager or director for the actors to ready themselves for the opening of a scene.

Principal Role – A primary or chief character.

Props – Anything that is handled, used or carried by an actor that is not considered to be part of the scenery or costuming. Personal props are props that can be kept in an actor's costume. Hand props are objects that are actually used by an actor.

Quick Change – A situation where an actor has only a few brief moment on the side of the stage to hastily change from one costume into another. This transition is generally made quicker with Velcro and zippers that are sewn into a costume.

Read Through – The initial cast reading(s) of script after the show has been fully cast.

Rehearsal – The practice working through some of the scenes from a script for an eventual public performance.

Right Stage – Actors right when facing the audience.

SAG – Screen Actors Guild.

Script – Copy of the text of a play, film, scene, or show.

Set Designer – Works with the director to create a background scenic look for the production, as well as any props to complete the realism of the overall theme. This artistic member of the team also keeps the scenery design within the budget of the theatre.

Sides – A section of the script used in an audition.

Slate – (1) Verbal identification before an audition. (2) A device used on film to identify shots for the editing process.

Soliloquy – When and actor is onstage speaking their thoughts aloud regardless of who may be listening.

Speed Through - Fast paced read through (generally without reading from text) of the entire cast to review lines.

Stage Manager – (SM) this is the member of the team who attends all rehearsals/performances and then calls the cues/runs the book for the show. Also sometimes known as a Stage Director, responsible for all aspects of a performance – often including but not limited to: checking prop placement, actors being in position and on time, sound cues, lighting cues, etc. **Assistant Stage Manager** – ASM - assists the SM

Strike – At the end of the run of a show, this is the process of disassembling the set, putting away all props, properly storing costumes, and cleaning up the theatre in general.

Supporting Role – Generally a less demanding role than a lead or principal role, but still quite memorable and/or detrimental to the plot.

Technical Director - In charge of the technical requirements of a production.

Technical Rehearsal or "Tech" – When scenes are assigned lighting cues, scenery cues, and sound cues –

among other technical aspects of the show that are necessary to make the production run smoothly. <u>Dry Tech</u> – without actors. <u>Wet Tech</u> – with actors present.

Title Role – The role in which you play the character that the title of the piece refers to.

Understudy – When a member of the cast is prepared to take over a principal role if needed.

Upstage – Closest to back wall ("up, up and away") and away from the audience.

Upstaging Yourself – When actors angle themselves upstage and away from the audience.

STAGE DIRECTIONS

UR	UC	UL
UP RIGHT	UP CENTER	UP LEFT
RC	**C**	**LC**
RIGHT CENTER	CENTER	LEFT CENTER
DR	**DC**	**DL**
DOWN RIGHT	DOWN CENTER	DOWN LEFT

Audience

RECOMMENDED READING

Adler, Stella. *The Art of Acting.* Applause Theatre & Cinema Books. New York. 2000.

Brown, D. W. *You Can Act!* Michael Wiese Productions. Studio City. 2009.

Caldarone, Marina & Maggie Lloyd-Williams. *Actions: The Actors' Thesaurus.* Drama Publishers. USA. 2004.

Meisner, Sanford & Dennis Longwell. *Sanford Meisner on Acting.* Random House, Inc. Toronto. 1987.

Salinsky, Tom & Deborah Frances-White. *The Improv Handbook.* The Continuum International Publishing Group Inc. New York. 2008.

Stanislavski, Constantin. *An Actor Prepares.* Routledge. New York. 2011.

Shurtleff, Michael. *Audition: Everything an Actor Needs to Know to Get the Part.* Walker Publishing Company, Inc. Ontario. 1978.

BIBLIOGRAPHY

Adler, Ronald B., Lawrence B. Rosenfeld, and Russell F. Proctor II. *Interplay: The Process of Interpersonal Communications.* Oxford University Press, Inc. New York. 2007.

Brown, D. W. *You Can Act!* Michael Wiese Productions. Studio City. 2009.

"History." *Stella Adler Studio of Acting.* 30 Oct. 2012. 15 Nov. 2012 <http://www.stellaadler.com/about/history/>.

"History." *The Lee Strasberg Theatre & Film Institute.* 28 Sept. 2012 <http://www.methodactingstrasberg.com/history>.

Meisner, Sanford and Dennis Longwell. *Sanford Meisner on Acting.* Random House, Inc. Toronto. 1987.

Salinsky, Tom & Deborah Frances-White. *The Improv Handbook.* The Continuum International Publishing Group Inc. New York. 2008.

Shelokhonov, Steve. "Biography for Konstantin Stanislavski." *IMDb.* 22 Aug. 2012 <http://www.imdb.com/name/nm2507427/bio>.

Shurtleff, Michael. *Audition: Everything an Actor Needs to Know to Get the Part.* Walker Publishing Company, Inc. Ontario. 1978.

Stanislavski, Constantin. *An Actor Prepares.* Routledge. New York. 2011.

Tucker, Patrick and Christine Ozanne. *Award Monologues for Women.* Routledge. New York. 2007.

ACKNOWLEDGMENTS

Thanks to following people who made this book possible through help, insight, and/or encouragement:

Jared, Jada and Xander, Pamela and Jim Kercher, Michele Willis, Naomi Owen, Bruce and Margaret Bortz, Russell and Gloria Fellman, Carol and Tim Maher, Lindsey "Super Cousin" Seltzer and Rick Seltzer, Kristen Zellner, Celena Romero, Nicole Pedrick, Kym DeFour and Sheri Mitchell, Kay and Louis Walker, Dean Bortz, Sandi and Dan Einsla, Rick and Cyndy Hillegass, Celeste, Bill, Tim, Steve, Brian, Scott, Sean, Geoff, Christian, Josh, Chad Boushell, Kristi Curtis, Ellen Rauch for your dedicated, enthusiastic, and careful reading, Mark Hildebrand for close reading and detailed editing, Christy Dunbar for faithful reading, and Sally Stotter for your encouragement and reading.

ABOUT THE AUTHOR

Tesia Nicoli grew up knowing she wanted to be an actress. In the early years of her life, her theatrical desires were expressed through an overabundance of "shows" she would produce for any family member. High school plays and the occasional acting gig in college still did not satisfy her acting bug. She eventually earned a degree in communications and professional writing. Nicoli took as many acting classes as possible early in her career, and she landed her first role in a community theatre production after attending her first acting class. She has since worked extensively in theatre, film, television, and commercial work.

Nicoli has written twelve plays, three of which have been produced on stage. Over the years she has worked as a talent scout, location scout, scriptwriter, assistant director, director, acting coach, and production assistant. Nicoli has also recorded numerous voice over projects for commercials and eLearning courses. She began teaching acting classes in 2006, and has since continued to teach a variety of drama-related courses such as: *Focus on Film*, *Auditions & Monologues*, *Acting: On Camera Critique*, *Improvisation Basics and Beyond*, *Acting for Youth*, and *Acting, Drama & Performance*. She also teaches private lessons to children and adults looking for individual assistance and guidance. In 2012, Nicoli founded *The Acting Edge*, a social networking place for people interested in the acting industry. *The Acting Edge* also produces informational videos on various acting topics, which you can find through Nicoli's website: www.tesianicoli.com. Nicoli lives west of Allentown, Pennsylvania with her husband, two children, and two cats.

Made in the USA
Charleston, SC
27 January 2013